Climber's Guide: Riverside Quarry
Second Edition

Louie Anderson

Climber's Guide: Riverside Quarry
Second Edition

ISBN: 978-0-9766630-0-3

Copyright 2012 Louie Anderson
All rights reserved.
Printed in China

No part of this book may be reproduced in any way without the express written permission of the author.

All uncredited photos by the author, except for nature photos by the author,
Richard and Robert Heinrich.

Front Cover: Valarie Heredia on *Hanging by a Thread* (12b)

Rear Cover: Quarry panorama Photo: Mark Ackley
Louie Anderson on *Taboo* (12c) Photo: Perri Nguyen
Chris Lindner on *Enigma* (13b)

Contact the author:

Louie Anderson
PO Box 411 • Silverado, CA 92676-0411 • louieanderson@live.com

CLIMBING IS DANGEROUS !

The user of this book accepts all risks associated with the activities described herein. Climbing carries great risk for injury or death. The information offered in this book shall in no way supersede one's own judgment and/or common sense when it comes to assessing the dangers involved with a particular climb and whether or not the information presented here is accurate for the situation at hand. All protection information, difficulties and descriptions provided in this book should be treated as suggestions, not absolutes. The author, editors, publishers, land owners or land managers accept no liability for any injuries incurred from using this book or the climbs described herein.

Tony Sartin On Burly Boogie (13a)

Climber's Guide: Riverside Quarry

Second Edition

Louie Anderson

Table of Contents

Mike Heredia on Stemsation (10a)

Table of Contents

Acknowledgements	6
Location And Driving Times	12
Quarry	16
Wildlife	16
Weather And Season	17
Amenities	18
Access And Conduct	21
Area History	37
Developer Profiles	47
Slab City	52
Slab City Left	54
Slab City Center	60
Slab City Right	64
Metro Sector	69
Left of the Roof	72
Flesh and Blood Profile	75
Raging Raptor Profile	76
Trundle Trophy Profile	80
Roof Area	83
Nostalgia Profile	84
Hanging by a Thread Profile	88
The Zone Profile	90
American Dream Profile	94
Right of the Roof	98
Torture Machine Area	105
Tangerine Dream Profile	108
Slander Sector	110
Rubble Row	113
King Pin Profile	116
Slide Zone	121
The Tall Wall	124
The Shield	127
Enigma Profile	128
Anger Management Area	133
Taboo Area	139
Taboo Profile	142
Violator Profile	144
Forbidden Fruit Profile	150
The Alcove	153
Schoolhouse Rock	158
The Fun Factory	162
Fun Factory Profile	166
Agony Arch Area	168
Quarry Grade Dozens	172
Quarry Routes By Quality	174
Index	184
Advertisements	188
About the Author	199

Acknowledgements

Gray Fox — Photo: Richard Heinrich

Acknowledgements

No climbing guidebook has ever been written without the support and assistance of many people and groups whose names are not shown on the cover. This book is certainly no exception. Huge efforts have been made by many people, and I greatly appreciate everything that all have done to help and support me along the way while researching and preparing this book for printing. In no particular order, the following people are worthy of specific mention:

Grahm Doe – for seeing past the choss and committing to the task at hand when the cliff was still full of loose rock, and for keeping me motivated when that task often seemed daunting. Your lines are some of the best at the crag, and I only wish you were around to see the culmination of our shared vision.

Brent Webster – for being part of the work party from day one. While his name isn't found attached to many of the routes, rest assured that Brent was there for much of what transpired. Your optimism and energy are contagious and much appreciated.

Gary Henning – for your continued support over the years. Thank you for The Alcove and for your additions elsewhere along the cliff. Thank you also for your help in developing the Fun Factory.

Richard Jensen and Mark Smith – for all of your initial work developing climbing at the Quarry. For taking the time to show me around and for taking me under your wings, offering encouragement and education. Finally, for writing your 1982 guidebook that first brought the Quarry to the eyes of the general climbing public.

Mark Maynard – for being the first to truly explore the sport climbing potential of the area, and for showing us that even granite can feature huge pockets.

Andre Kiryanov, Richard Heinrich, Robert Heinrich, Perri Nguyen, Chris Miller and all the other photographers – for allowing me to use your images to supplement the information in this book. The presentation of that information is much richer thanks to your work.

All of the climber in the action photos – for letting me (and others) shoot you on the routes. I've

Acknowledgements

tried to spotlight some of the climbers who've had a steady presence at the cliff over the years and to give you a little recognition. Thank you for your continued presence at the Quarry and for helping me to present to the readers what some of the particular routes look like. The quantity of photos in this edition gives a much better visual representation to readers not familiar with the area than anything I wrote could possibly achieve with words.

Will Gove, Dan Delange, Steve Shifflet, Alex Thayer and many others – for all of your feedback on the difficulty and quality of the routes in the Quarry. I really wanted to get a much more complete grade consensus in this edition of the guide. While I received input from many dozens of local climbers, you have all been extremely helpful and I appreciate your comments and opinions.

Valarie Heredia – for your love, perseverance, and support, but mainly for being such a wonderful partner.

Matt Callender – for your friendship and for holding my rope so many times, and at so many areas, over the years. Also, for being an early supporter of our efforts at the Quarry.

Bill Leventhal – for your steady presence at the crag, and for bringing so many of your friends that may not have come otherwise.

Chris, Elke and Tom Lindner – the first family of SoCal sport climbing. Thank you Chris for being an inspiration, and for being a genuinely nice guy. Elke and Tom: thank you for your support and for being such regulars for so many seasons at the Quarry – I hope to see you back again soon.

Fixe Hardware and Mad Rock – for making the hardware used on many of the Quarry climbs. Thanks for keeping us all safe.

Tony Sartin – for your friendship and support. It's always nice to run into you at the Quarry and elsewhere. You're one of the most consistent climbers I know and always full of positive energy.

Nino Guagliano – for making the hard routes look easy. I especially am grateful for your ratings feedback on some of the harder routes at the Quarry. It's difficult to gain consensus on routes that have often seen only a handful of ascents. As such, your opinions are very valuable.

Advertisers – for your financial support of this book. Please look at the advertisements beginning on page 187. If you like this book, please support these companies. Their financial commitments made its publication possible.

Alex and Laura Bennett – for all of your creative energy and efforts. This book looks far better for your assistance. Thank you also for your friendship.

To all that have bolted and helped to develop climbing areas here and abroad - few climbers realize the massive amount of time, energy and money that you have donated to broaden our climbing options. Thank you one and all!

And finally, to all of the Quarry climbers – it's been wonderful to meet all of you from time to time at the crag. Climbing is one of those rare activities where the camaraderie and welcoming sense of family seems universal. I've benefitted greatly from knowing you all, and seeing you enjoying the routes and the area brings me great joy. Please be safe and continue to treat each other well…

Preface

Ashley Duran on Flexercise (10b)

Preface

This book is long overdue – for that I apologize. A huge effort has been made to solicit and incorporate the feedback and opinions of those climbers that frequent the area. The sheer volume of information that has been received has made this book a massive undertaking. I'm very pleased with the consensus opinions offered in this edition. Some ratings have changed (both difficulty and quality) and these changes are the direct result of the feedback I've received. When the last edition to this guide was released, many of the routes described had not previously been published and the ratings offered were based on the opinions of a very limited number of individuals. Many of the harder routes had literally seen just a handful of ascents. The information offered here is based on a much broader consensus. I had also envisioned this edition to be a huge step up in quality. I wanted it to be printed in full color and to have far more action photos and other added features to make it entertaining and interesting to read and use. Included now are tick lists for different grade levels. I have also taken a survey of many of the regular Quarry climbers and from that have compiled a list of the fourteen routes those surveyed felt were worthy of extra attention. Each of these routes has a special profile, offering expanded information and action photos. I wanted to give recognition to those that have helped to make the Quarry what it is today and have offered a short profile on three of the other climbers that have had a hand in the development of the Quarry and it's routes. Finally, the history section has been updated and expanded as I have found more information about the climbing activities at the crag. All of this has taken time to achieve, but I hope that the final product seems worth the wait to all of you.

I have also made the difficult decision to limit the book to include only the free climbing options in the Quarry. This was a very hard decision for me, as my own Quarry experience was founded in aid climbing. Through my adventures on the cliff, I became friends with those involved in developing the crag as an aid climbing area. By not describing those routes, I feel as though I am in some way doing a disservice to them and to their efforts. The simple truth is that many of the original aid routes followed lines of loose and flexing features. The lack of structural integrity in those features is what provided the allure and associated difficulty of those aid lines. Several of the routes were never published and during the cleaning of the walls for sport climbing many of the features climbed by those routes were removed in an attempt to make the cliff safer and more solid. Many other lines were wandering or traversing in nature and are now criss-crossed with sport climbs. Some respect was given to the known aid climbs when establishing sport climbs, but this was not always the case and many routes were lost as a result. Because so few of the aid climbs remain in a climbable state, the decision was made to not include them at all. However, the Quarry's aid climbing history is rich. In many ways it laid the groundwork for everything that has followed. Mark Smith has written a great summation of the history of this era and it has been included in the Introduction section of this book. I hope that you all take the time to read it and appreciate all that came before the current version of the Quarry that we all associate with and enjoy today.

No one could have predicted the renewed interest in a crag that has seen climbing activity for better than 50 years, but here we are. In recent years, the area has seen a huge increase in climbing activity and the number of climbers visiting on a regular basis. Part of that has to do with recent new route additions, but I believe that the greater catalyst has been that more climbers are now aware of the wonderful climbing options that the Quarry has to offer. The quality of the rock, the variety of movement found on the climbs, the broad range of difficulties available, and the short approach all overshadow the less than aesthetic surroundings. The Quarry will never be described

Preface

as offering a pristine wilderness experience, but the quality of the climbing more than makes up for that.

My first visit to the Quarry came in 1978 with a crazy Vietnam Vet named Jack Hughes. Jack was a friend of my dad and largely responsible for some of my early climbing adventures. We set up some scary topropes somewhere on the right fringe of what's now called the *Taboo Area* and *The Alcove*. Miraculously, for our skills at the time, none of our anchors pulled and we had a lot of fun climbing the short, clean slabs. We played on some of the taller faces, but didn't really push our limits too much.

I didn't return until about 1983 when I began to become more interested in aid climbing. At that time the Quarry was the scene of an underground aid climbing boom. I nailed my way out the fun traverse of Romp, and met the area's prime developers, Richard Jensen and Mark Smith. These two were regularly nailing and heading up the rotten seams and blast lines of the crag, claiming that they were the perfect mental training ground for the heady wall climbing found in Yosemite Valley. The pair went on to establish the recently repeated *Wings of Steel* - A5 (on El Capitan) and repeat what was considered at the time to be the hardest wall in the world, *Sea of Dreams* - A5 (also on El Capitan). Taking this into consideration, I imagine they knew what they were talking about. Over the next several years they showed me the better lines in the Quarry and I enjoyed practicing my piton and heading skills, as well as polishing my rope management and freeing a few of the cleaner cracks.

Jump forward several years. It's now the early 90's and I'm becoming more and more of a sport climber; focusing most of my energy on developing new routes. Several times between then and now I had visited the Quarry and walked along the base of its walls; knowing that they would probably offer good climbing, but also knowing that the work to clean them up would be extreme. Much of that work has now been done and I'm pleased to say that the Quarry of today is a much safer place to climb than it once was. Climbers have organized area cleanups and have collected and disposed of literally tons of rubbish and debris. Graffiti has been removed, trails have been developed and maintained, everyone is now parking outside the Quarry property, and generally the area is a much nicer place to be.

If you're looking for aid and traditional climbing, you'll find a handful of great routes here. Sport climbing, however, is the main offering of the area and the sport routes are where the Quarry really shines. This guidebook describes (338) routes ranging from easy 5th class to 5.14. While most of the routes lie in the 5.11 to 5.12 range, there really is something for everyone at the Quarry. Many people have described the Quarry as an "outdoor gym" and I would have to admit that in many ways it is one. It certainly is a great place to get stronger and to expand your climbing abilities. In fact a series of injuries and some turmoil in my personal life have led to a much lower level of climbing ability for me personally than what I have enjoyed in the past. As a result I am now rediscovering the Quarry's more moderate routes, and enjoying them thoroughly, as I fight my way back through the grades once again. I hope that you too can find inspiration at the Quarry to push yourself and to improve on the huge roster of quality routes that it has to offer.

Enjoy the climbing and be safe out there.

Louie Anderson

January 2012

Introduction

Louie Anderson on Seduction (12d)
Photo: Matt Hulet

You are reading the latest edition of the first guidebook devoted to the climbing found in the Riverside Quarry. The first edition was written by Richard Jensen and Mark Smith, and released in 1982. That book was updated and a second edition was released in 2005. Since that time there have been several routes added to the crag. This guide updates information offered in those first editions and presents information on all subsequent routes. It has been painstakingly researched for your enjoyment. Please read the entire introduction.

The Quarry is located in the small town of Sunnyslope, at the border of one of its residential areas. The surrounding area is a popular recreation venue for multiple user groups. Don't be surprised to see trail runners, horseback riders, dirt bikers and other off road enthusiasts, paint ballers, mountain bikers, BASE jumpers, recreational walkers, trash collectors or lovers looking for a midday urban rendezvous. Most of these people are used to seeing climbers at the Quarry and so far everyone seems to get along.

The routes found in the Quarry are unique in their offerings to the regional climbing community. Long routes are the norm, with the average length being 100 feet. There are a few shorter routes, and a few that are much longer, including some multi-pitch lines. While the length of these routes offer a great training venue for those looking to improve their stamina and overall endurance, don't be discouraged as most of the routes feature several good rests (often no hands) with which to keep the pump at bay. Learning to take advantage of these is the secret to success at the Quarry.

The rock is good quality granite that is surprisingly well featured. This is thanks to the blasting performed during the initial quarrying operations. You would be hard pressed to find a natural granite cliff anywhere that offered the same proliferation and variety of features as what you will find here. On all but the hardest routes, the overhangs and bulges will usually reward climbers with positive features and gymnastic climbing moves. The developers have gone to great lengths to remove all loose rock from the routes and to make the base areas clean and comfortable. Please do your part to continue this effort.

Location

Location And Driving Times

The Quarry is located just north of the 60 freeway and South of the 10 freeway. It's visible when driving through the town of Sunnyslope on the 60 freeway and the driving approach is fairly obvious.

From the 60 freeway:

Exit the Valley Way off-ramp. When heading east on the freeway, you will have to turn left onto Mission Boulevard to reach Valley Way. Once you reach Valley Way head north (toward the mountains). You will pass through a couple of traffic signals before reaching a signal at the intersection with Sierra Avenue. Turn right here. Pass through a residential tract with block walls on either side of the street. When the block wall on your left ends, you will see the Quarry cliff line on your left. There is no parking or driving allowed on the Quarry property. Although rare, there have been instances of vehicle break-ins, so it's generally best and safest to park your vehicle inside the residential area across from the Quarry. If you turn right onto Donner Way and then again right on Upton Court, there is a large area of curbside parking where the are no homes or driveways. There are a few trail and dirt road options when entering the Quarry. See trail map on page 10 for more information.

From the 10 freeway:

Exit the Sierra Avenue off-ramp and head south (away from the mountains). You will pass through a couple of traffic signals before driving up and over a large hill. As you crest the hill you will see the Quarry directly ahead and below you. Continue on Sierra Avenue when you reach the intersection with Armstrong at the bottom of the hill. Pass through a residential tract with block walls on either side of the street. When the block wall on your left ends, you will see the Quarry cliff line on your left. There is no parking or driving allowed on the Quarry property. Although rare, there have been instances of vehicle break-ins, so it's generally best and safest to park your vehicle inside the residential area across from the Quarry. If you turn right onto Donner Way and then again right on Upton Court, there is a large area of curbside parking where there are no homes or driveways. There are a few trail and dirt road options when entering the Quarry. See trail map on page 10 for more information.

The climbs found in the Quarry are approached from the parking area by following a handful of easy to moderate hiking trails. There are a number of splinter trails leading to all sections of the cliff. Please do your part to keep the trails clear, maintained, and well defined.

Location

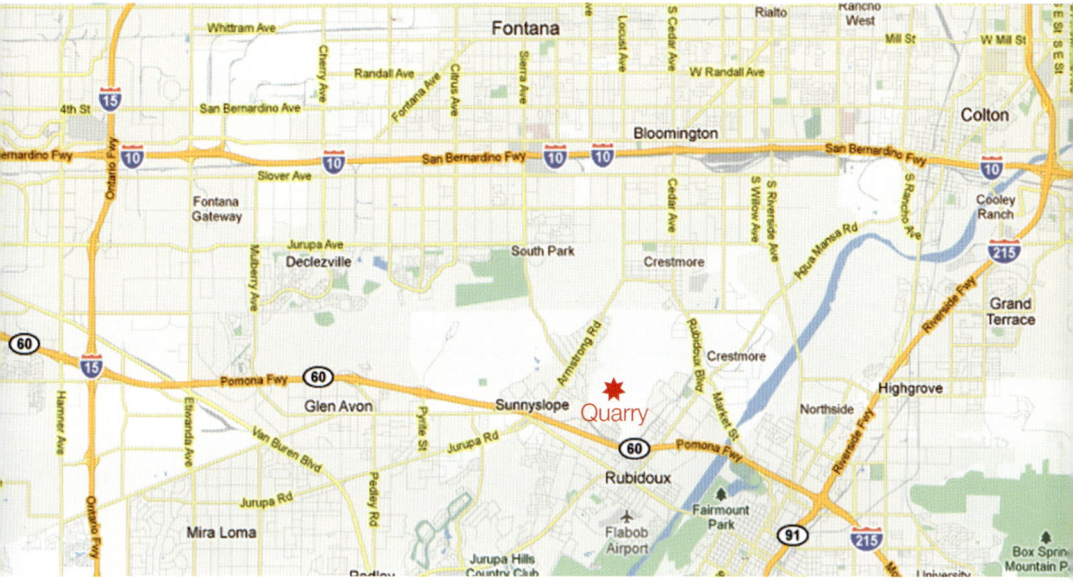

Area Map

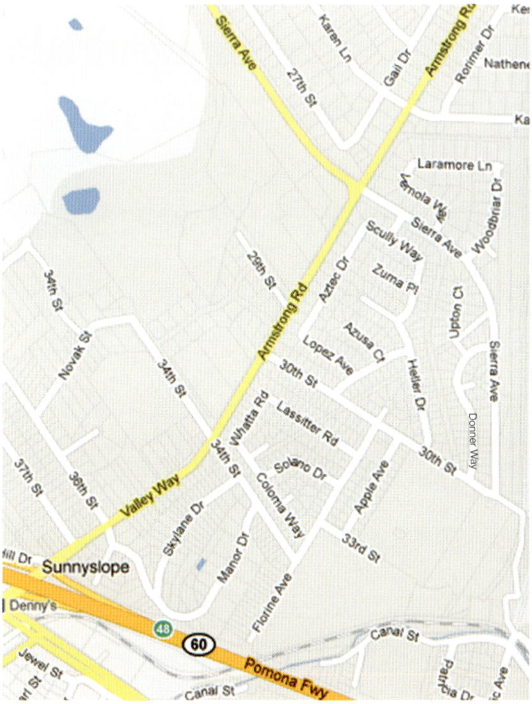

Neighborhood Map

Aerial View

Aerial View: © 2011 Google Imagery, © 2011 County of San Bernardino, DigitalGlobe, GeoEye, U. S. Geological Survey, USDA Farm Service Agency, Map data: © 2011 Google

Maps: © 2011 Google

Location

Driving Times:

The central location of the Quarry to Southern California climbers is one of its greatest attributes. Given below are approximate driving times from larger cities and regional climbing destinations.

Larger Cities:

Riverside – 10 minutes

San Diego – 1 hour

Orange County – 30 to 60 minutes

Los Angeles – 1 hour

Santa Barbara – 2 hours

Victorville – 1 hour

Regional Climbing Areas:

Joshua Tree – 1 to 1 ½ hours

Tahquitz / Suicide Rocks – 1 hour

Frustration Creek – 40 minutes

Big Bear Areas – 1 to 1 ½ hours

Mt. Williamson – 1 ½ hours

Devil's Punchbowl – 1 hour

High Desert – 1 to 1 ½ hours

New Jack City – 1 ½ hours

Santa Monica Mountain Areas – 1 ½ hours

The Pinnacles – 5 hours

Yosemite Valley – 7 ½ hours

Red Rocks – 4 hours

Owens River Gorge – 4 to 5 hours

Travis Nelson on Nostalgia (11c) Photo: Andre Kiryanov

James Saito on Weight of the World (13c)

Wildlife

Quarry Wildlife

The Quarry is home to a surprising amount of wildlife, given its urban location. Perhaps the most prevalent are the thousands of swallows that live in the crag's cracks and flake systems, which come out in the early evening to feed. There are also Red Tail Hawks, and a handful of Barn Owls and Pigeons rounding out the bird population. Bats are often seen too in the evenings, but are rarely seen during the daytime. A wide assortment of squirrels and field mice live in the talus at the base of the cliff, and it's not uncommon to see wild rabbits and coyotes in the flat lands below the talus slope. There are also a variety of lizards and snakes and, while it is rare to see them, Rattlesnakes do live in the area as well.

Climbers and other area user groups interact with all of these animals on a regular basis. The true mascots of the Quarry, however, are Sally and Scruffy. They are a pair of Gray Foxes that live in the talus caves below the main cliff. They have been seen at the cliff since at least the early 2000's, but it's assumed that a fox population of some sort has lived in the area for much longer. Gray Foxes are monogamous, and these two are a couple. It's easy to tell the two apart, as Scruffy is slightly larger and has a tear in his right ear. There have been a handful of litters born to the pair and many of their pups may now be preparing to have litters of their own.

The Quarry foxes are fairly active in the early morning, but tend to go back to their dens during the heat of the day. They do not generally show a lot of fear when around people, but please respect the fact that they are wild animals and give them their space. While some climbers give them water, please do not feed them. They have plenty of prey in the area, and we should respect their normal dietary patterns.

Weather And Season

Jack Marshall on Leviathan (11d)

The Quarry's cliffs are in the shade during the first part of the day allowing for cool temperature climbing and redpoint conditions. This shade also allows for climbing during the hottest of summer months. During the heat of summer this shade usually lasts until about 12:30 p.m. or so (depending on the wall you're interested in). During the winter most walls go into the sun about 11:30 a.m.

Winter mornings can be quite cold. In fact many climbers will start the day in long pants and either fleece or down jackets, only to finish the day in shorts and wearing no shirt. Winter is really the prime time to visit the area if you plan to spend the entire day climbing, with the fall and spring months offering only slightly warmer temperatures.

Summer temperatures can be well into the 90's and above, so if you choose to climb in the afternoon – be prepared. Bring plenty of water (try freezing your bottle the night before) and apply sunscreen as needed. The broken boulders and talus at the base of the walls offer shady escapes from the sun and heat, and many routes offer shady belay stations at their base.

Be aware that due to the unnatural exposure of the Quarry walls, that many of them will seep for a short time after heavy rainstorms. Most routes will usually dry out very quickly (usually after no more than a day or so of sunshine) and not all walls or routes are affected by this seepage. Another thing to realize is that some routes will get a light dusting of runoff sand from the top of the cliff during rain and windstorms. If you climb immediately after a rain, don't be surprised if some of the edges and ledges have a fine layer of grit. It's usually not enough to make holds unusable, and a quick brushing of the route will bring it back to normal. If confronted with dusty holds please do other climbers a favor and take the time to brush them off.

Amenities

Food:

The Quarry is conveniently located off major freeways. As such, the regular assortment of fast food, convenience, coffee and liquor establishments are all readily available. The closest food options are at the off-ramp areas of the 60 and 10 freeways.

The only convenient option, differing from the usual franchises, is TJ Tacos, located just north of the 60 freeway at 3612 Valley Way. They are located across the street and just north of the AMPM location. This "hole in the wall" offers traditional Mexican food, specializing in street tacos, burritos and tortas. Prices are low and the food is great.

Camping:

There are no convenient camping options, as the Quarry is located in a metropolitan area, with developed communities and commercial districts for miles around. There are discount hotels in the area that will surely have vacancies should you require lodging. The closest options are:

Motel 6
6830 Valley Way, Riverside, CA 92509
(951) 681-6666
Located just south of the 60 freeway, on the left.

Circle Inn Motel
9220 Granite Hill Drive, Riverside, CA 92509
(951) 360-1132
Located just north of the 60 freeway, at the Pedley Road off-ramp.

Motel 6
10195 Sierra Avenue, Fontana, CA 92335
(909) 823-8686

Located just north of the 10 freeway, on the right. There are several other hotels in the City of Fontana along Valley, which parallels the 10 freeway at the Sierra Avenue off-ramp.

Amenities

Climbing Gear:

The closest retailers that sell climbing gear are REI and Sport Chalet. There are three locations within a short drive from the Quarry:

REI
12218 Foothill Blvd, Rancho Cucamonga, CA 91739
(909) 646-8360 Approximately 6 miles away

Sport Chalet
12449 Foothill Blvd., Rancho Cucamonga, CA 91739
(909) 987-4321
Approximately 5 miles away

Sport Chalet
13041 Peyton Drive, Chino Hills, CA 91709
(909) 627-8996
Approximately 12 miles away

Several of the climbing gyms listed on the next page also sell basic consumables (chalk, etc.), with some offering a larger variety of items.

Andrea Pesce on Salutations (11b)

Amenities

Climbing Gyms:

There are a number of climbing gyms in southern California. Those located within an hour of the Quarry include the following (in order of proximity):

Hangar 18
6935 Arlington Avenue
Riverside, CA 92503
(951) 359-5040 • www.climbhangar18.com

Thresh Hold Climbing and Fitness
2111 Iowa Avenue, Unit A
Riverside, CA 92507
(951) 742-8479 • www.climbth.com

Hangar 18
256 Stowell Street, Unit A
Upland, CA 91786
(909) 931-5991 • www.climbhangar18.com

Rock City
5100 E. La Palma Avenue, Unit 108 -109
Anaheim Hills, CA 92870
(714) 777-4884 • www.rockcityclimbing.com

Vital Climbing Gym
29990 Technology Drive, Unit 22
Murrieta, CA 92563
(951) 251-4814 • www.vitalclimbinggym.com

The Bullet Hole
15315 Cholame Road, Unit D
Victorville, CA 92392
(760) 245-3307 • www.thebullethole.net

Arcadia Rock Climbing (the ARC)
305 N. Santa Anita Blvd, Unit B
Arcadia CA 91006
(626) 294-9111 • www.arcadiarockclimbing.com

Rockreation
1300 Logan Avenue,
Costa Mesa, CA 92626
(714) 556-7625 • www.rockreation.com

Dan Delange on The Ultimate (12d)
Photo: Willard Gove

Access And Conduct

Access Information:

The Quarry is privately owned, but has a longstanding history (more than 50 years) of climber access. This does not mean that we have carte blanche to act and do whatever we want while climbing at the Quarry. Please realize the potential of your actions to impact access, act responsibly and follow these guidelines:

- Respect the land managers, neighbors and Sheriffs. Do your best to interact in a friendly manner and be sure to wave or say "hello" when you see them. Anything that can be done to keep our interactions friendly can only help in the long run.

- Try not to disrupt neighbors and other recreational groups you come across. This is a rather broad guideline, but one that can be broken down to include radios, loud yelling and screaming, driving recklessly, completely overtaking an area to where others won't feel welcome and other similar actions. It's always best that if any report gets back to land managers about climbers, that it be a positive one. Maintain a low profile.

- Don't leave trash. Whether it's yours or not - pick it up. This one action can make a huge difference. Applying this to the Quarry as a whole is not very realistic, but do your best to keep the base of the routes, access trails and parking areas clean. Don't get discouraged; simply take it one piece at a time. Before you know it the area will be spotless and continued upkeep will be easy.

- If you need to retreat from a route, leave a biner or screwlink behind instead of webbing. Not only will it be safer for the next climber on the route, it also creates a less obvious eyesore for other area users and land managers. Likewise keep chalk use to a minimum and wash or brush off all tick marks and excessive chalk when done with a route.

- Dispose of your bodily waste properly. Go at least 200 feet away from climbs and trails, and bury any solid waste. Pack out your toilet paper in a plastic bag and try not to reuse areas in order to prevent foul odors.

- Volunteer for local cleanup days and other service projects and make sure that you are identified as a climber.

Conduct:

Our sport is made up of many different types of people, with many different attitudes and approaches to their climbing. No two individuals will bring the same thing to the crag and we will all benefit or suffer by the choices that each individual climber makes. With this in mind, please abide by the following guidelines when climbing in the Quarry:

Access & Conduct

- If you bring your dog, please keep an eye on his actions. Most climbers will not mind an unleashed dog as long as it is well behaved and its owner is attentive to its actions. If your dog is not friendly or is not "crag trained", perhaps it would be best to leave it at home.

- Most climbers are drawn to climbing as an outdoor activity, where the natural surroundings, wildlife and serenity are as important as the climbing itself. Keep this in mind if you are fond of bringing a radio to the crag. If you do bring a radio and are climbing near others, ask if they would mind you listening to it at an acceptable volume. If they don't mind—thank them. If they do mind—respect their wishes and leave it off or wear headphones. Even if you're alone, realize that sounds carry in the Quarry. Respect the adjacent homeowners and keep the volume down.

- On a similar note, if you are prone to screaming and/or throwing tantrums after a failed attempt, realize that your actions are affecting the experience of those around you and that they probably do not appreciate the scene.

- Climbing is about camaraderie and I'm sure that we've all felt the surge of adrenaline as our friends on the ground shout their encouragement. Feel free to do the same to other climbers at the crag (regardless of whether they are a part of your party or not). Likewise if you know a piece of vital beta that might help a climber on a given route, and they don't mind hearing it (ask first) give them a hand by sharing the beta.

- If you're waiting for a belay or see someone else that needs a belay, offer to partner up for a route. Many new partnerships have begun this way and everybody gets more climbing time in the day by eliminating unwanted "down time." Also be quick to allow others to top-rope on your route and don't hesitate to ask others if they mind your using their top-rope.

- Unless you are the only person that is going to be climbing a given route, clip into the anchors with quickdraws and lower off of these. This will eliminate wear on the anchors and substantially increase their life span. When the last climber is set to lower off of the route, it's very easy for him/her to clean the quickdraws and to lower directly off the anchors and/or rappel.

- After climbing a route take the time to brush off any holds that have an accumulation of chalk. This will allow the next climber on the route to get a better grip on the hold and will limit unsightly and greasy chalk buildup. This is especially necessary on extremely popular routes or after extended work sessions. Only use a nylon or natural bristled brush. Never use a metal brush to clean off holds, as it will remove the texture from the hold and polish the rock. On a similar note, if you feel the need to mark blind holds or key "sweet spots" with a tick mark, take the time to wash it off when you're done. Many climbers do not like the visual impact that a route full of tick marks presents and onsight climbers may feel cheated by the additional information (correct or incorrect) that they offer.

- If you feel the need to retreat from a route before reaching the anchors please leave behind a carabiner or screwlink as opposed to a piece of webbing. This will create less of a visual impact and will insure that the next climber on the route will still be able to clip into the hanger and/or your carabiner.

Access & Conduct

- Some routes feature carabiners at the anchors. These have been provided for your convenience. Please realize this and do not remove them. Also, never remove quickdraws, ropes or other items off of routes or projects. These have been left intentionally and have not been abandoned. Leaving quickdraws on a project (whether it be a new route or simply an established route that a climber is trying to redpoint) is an accepted practice and the removal of these items can be viewed as nothing less than theft. If there are quickdraws on a route that you would like to attempt (and the route is not a new route project) feel free to clip into the quickdraws in place. Just remember to leave them when you are done with the route.

- In regards to quickdraws left on routes: please only do this if you are actively working on redpointing a route. The cliff at the Quarry is not steep enough to warrant leaving permanent quickdraws to assist in cleaning the routes. If there is a hanger on your project that is difficult to install the draw on during a redpoint attempt, you may want to leave a quickdraw at that clip temporarily. Please remember, however to remove it once you are done with the route.

- Please do not install permanent quickdraws (i.e.: chain draws) on the climbs in the Quarry. These are often installed on steep or traversing routes at some sport cliffs to aid in the cleaning of the draws from the route after it has been led. None of the climbs at the Quarry are steep enough or traverse enough to warrant their installation. Further, they are an eyesore to other area users. On a similar note, if you are working to redpoint a climb and feel that a particular clip is difficult enough that you would like to leave a draw in place until you have succeeded on your redpoint, please remove the draw after your success, or when you choose to no longer work on the climb.

- Respect any project with a red tag. The routes in the Quarry have been developed by a limited number of individuals investing their own energy, money and time. Due to the nature of the cliff, establishing a new route requires an immense amount of work. Stealing their projects is an insult to them and their efforts to provide additional climbing options for you, and shows a severe lack of appreciation for all that these people have donated to the climbing community. Realize also that these red tag rarely mean that the route is too difficult for the developer and that he cannot climb it. More often they mean that the developer has not yet finished cleaning off the loose and dangerous rock from the climb. It's really a matter of safety to stay off these routes until the red tag disappears.

- Occasionally a red tag will mark a route that is in the midst of maintenance work. As loose rock is found on existing routes, it sometimes requires some maintenance to remove this loose rock and make the route safe again. In this case, the tag will be removed once the work has been completed.

- If you are climbing on a route and come across a loose hold, you have two choices. If you can safely remove the loose rock please do so. However, if you cannot safely remove the rock, or consider it crucial for the route, please mark it with a chalked "X." This will help alert other climbers to the fact that it is loose and will serve as notice that the route is in need of some maintenance.

- Often times, plants will grow on the cliff face. When you encounter a plant on a route you are climbing, please remove it. If allowed to continue growth, the plant's roots will expand and pry rock away from the main wall, loosening holds and making routes unsafe over time.

Access & Conduct

- All of the routes described in this guide are approached on 100% volunteer maintained trails. Do your part to keep the trails clean and clear. Pick up all trash that you see (whether it's yours or not) and don't be afraid to reinforce loose sections of trail or to improve them as needed. Feel free to trim or remove plants as needed if they are encroaching on the trails, and help to keep the main trails bordered with rocks to better identify them. Keep your ears open for information on designated crag clean up and trail work days and don't hesitate to volunteer to help out.

- There are no bathroom facilities in the Quarry. If you need to go to the bathroom please walk far away from the climbing area and off of the trails before relieving yourself. Bury solid waste and pack out your toilet paper in a plastic bag. Try not to use the same areas that others before you have used in order to limit foul odors.

BASE jumper and climber sharing The Alcove — Photo: Robert Heinrich

Safety And Hazards

Safety Concerns:

Many of the routes described in this guide are sport climbing routes. There is a common misconception regarding sport climbing - that it is a completely safe endeavor. While it is safer than some other climbing pursuits it does still suffer from many of the same hazards and a few that seem more sport climbing related. Use your head, as most climbing accidents are a result of poor judgment and/or a hurried approach to the act. The following climbing related accidents are 100% avoidable:

- Failing to tie-in properly. People get sidetracked and either forget to complete their knot or tie in to the incorrect part of their harness. Get in the habit of checking your knot before leaving the ground. It's a good idea to recheck your knot before lowering off a route as well.

- A similar mistake is made when the harness buckle is not doubled back. This is usually caused by the climber being distracted and simply forgetting to finish. It's a good idea to check your own buckle and that of your partner before leaving the ground.

- With the increased popularity of sport climbing and its convenient approach to climbing, the use of a Gri-Gri as a belay device has become very common. Gri-Gris are excellent devices and once the initial adjustment period is over can offer a much better, safer and easier belay operation for both the climber and the belayer. This said, there have been a fair amount of accidents involving the rope being fed backwards through the device. When belaying check to make sure that you have fed the rope properly and give a quick upward tug on the climber's end of the rope to make sure that the device is catching properly before your partner leaves the ground.

- While every attempt has been made to offer correct route information in this guide, mistakes and/or misprints have probably occurred. Because of this whenever possible verify the correct number of bolts on a route in order to assure that you have enough quickdraws on your harness. Also, while almost all of the routes in this guide have fixed anchors at the end of the route, some of them are "closed" anchor systems where you will need an extra couple of draws in order to attach to the system. Prepare for this when applicable by carrying extra draws. Nothing is worse than running out of draws before reaching the anchors or reaching the anchors and having nothing with which to attach to them.

- Most of the routes in the Quarry are long enough that they require a 60 meter rope to lower off and/or top-rope. Several of them are rope stretchers even when using a 60-meter rope. Pay attention to the route descriptions and use a long rope where instructed. Even on shorter routes it's a good practice to be aware of the amount of remaining rope when lowering another climber. If there's any doubt as to whether your rope is long enough, tie a knot in the ground end of the rope to prevent it from passing through your belay device.

Safety and Hazards

- There are a handful of extended routes at the Quarry. These are routes that are longer than 100 feet (usually between 100 and 150 feet). The process for descending from the top of these routes is called lower-pull-lower (L-P-L). Basically, the climber will lower from the topmost anchors to lower anchors at the 100 foot level and clip in. He will then pull the rope and lower to the ground from these anchors. When required, this will be noted in the route descriptions.

- The rock found in the Quarry can sometimes be loose. Be aware of this and do not belay or stand below other climbers. If you are climbing and encounter loose rock warn anyone on the ground below you and then dislodge the rock so that it won't be a concern for future climbers. Even on popular and well-traveled routes, holds will occasionally break. As such, it may be wise to wear a helmet.

- The Quarry offers good cellular phone coverage. It is a good idea to carry your cellular phone with you in case of an accident.

Objective Hazards:

There are a couple of objective hazards found in the Quarry. Be prepared for either of them.

Rattlesnakes:

Rattlesnakes can occasionally be found in the Quarry. They can be identified primarily by the rattles on their tail, however sometimes snakes lose these. They can also be identified by their powerful body, thin neck and well-defined triangular or arrow shaped head. Their eyes are hooded and oval rather than round like nonpoisonous snakes. Especially in warm weather they will stretch across flat, exposed areas in order to soak up the heat of the sun. When not sunning, rattlesnakes can usually be found in areas of dense brush or jumbled, rocky areas.

It is a common belief that rattlesnakes are aggressive. This is entirely untrue. In most cases they will only attack if they feel threatened and have no options for escape. The actual act of "rattling" is meant to alert you to their presence and to offer a warning. If you hear this rattling, stop what you are doing and move away from the sound. Unless you have no escape route yourself, do not poke at the snake with a stick or throw rocks at it as this will only put the snake in a more defensive position where an attack is more likely.

Although you hear of several rattlesnake sightings, it is extremely uncommon to hear of bites. And less than 1/2% of those bitten die as a result of their bite. In fact, up to 60% of snake bites are what are known as a "dry bite," where no venom is released by the snake. If you watch your step and steer clear of snakes if and when you see them, you should have no problems with them whatsoever. Always give snakes the right of way.

Safety and Hazards

Brian Cullen on Control Freak (13a)

Safety and Hazards

What to do in case of a bite:

- Move away from the snake in order to prevent further bites.

- Remain calm and place the bitten limb in a comfortable position at a level slightly lower than the victim's heart.

- Look for the exact site of the bite (you should be able to see the fang punctures).

- If you have a Sawyer Pump Extractor®, or other suitable venom extractor (available at most larger sporting goods or hunting stores for about $10.00), select a cup size that covers both punctures and begin use (it's a good idea to read the instructions ahead of time).

- If you do not have a venom extractor, apply hard pressure to the puncture area with a clean cloth and tape in place with climbing or other adhesive tape.

- In either of the above first aid treatments, you should now wrap an ACE bandage or wide cloth strip around the bitten limb just above the puncture site. Wrap with approximately the same tightness that you would for a sprained ankle, but not too tightly. Check periodically for a pulse below your wrap to make sure that it is not too tight. If you are ever unable to find a pulse rewrap the bandage looser.

- Get to a hospital as soon as possible. Most available information suggests a time of one to one and a half hours from the time of the bite as being an acceptable time frame for best treatment options. Call ahead, if possible, and let them know that you are on the way, or that you need assistance. Have them make sure that they have antivenin on hand.

- **Call the California Poison Control System anytime, anyplace in California at 1-800-876-4766.**

What not to do in case of a bite:

- Don't apply a tourniquet.

- Don't apply ice or heat to the puncture site.

- Don't cut the puncture site.

- Don't use your mouth to suck out the venom.

- Don't give the victim drugs or alcohol.

- Don't apply electric shock.

- Don't remove the venom extractor or dressings until you are instructed to do so by a medical attendant.

- Don't attempt to capture or kill the snake. In all modern medical facilities the same antivenin is used.

Safety and Hazards

Sun Exposure:

Especially when climbing during the summer months, you can be exposed to direct sunlight and high temperatures for an extended period of time. Because of this it is a good idea to use a sufficiently strong enough sunscreen to prevent sunburn. Wear a hat and a long sleeve shirt if you are particularly susceptible to sunburn and try to follow the shade whenever possible.

With the heat comes the need to drink plenty of fluids. Make sure to bring enough water with you to the crag and stay well hydrated throughout the day. At the end of the day be sure to replenish you body with electrolyte drinks and/or additional water. Use the old urine test: if your urine is yellow you need more fluids, if it's clear you're doing just fine.

Medical Facilities:

The closest complete medical facility to the crag is:

Kaiser Permanente Hospital
9961 Sierra Ave., Fontana, CA 92335
(909) 427-5000 • (909) 427-6030 – Emergency

Directions:
Exit the Quarry and turn right onto Sierra Avenue. Cross Armstrong and go up and over the hill. Continue past the 10 freeway and turn right on Valley Boulevard (first traffic signal). The hospital will be on the left, on the northeast corner of Sierra Avenue and Valley Boulevard.

There are a number of additional medical facilities within a half hour drive of the Quarry. These include the following:

Corona Regional Medical Center
800 S Main Street, Corona, CA 91720
(951) 737-4343

Kaiser Permanente Hospital
10800 Magnolia, Riverside, CA 92505
(951) 353-2000

Loma Linda University Medical Center
11234 Anderson Street
Loma Linda, CA 92354
(800) 752-5999

Parkview Community Hospital
3865 Jackson, Riverside, CA 92503
(951) 688-2211

Riverside Community Hospital
4445 Magnolia Ave , Riverside, CA 92501
(951) 788-3000

In Case of Accident:

It is a good idea to carry and know how to use a basic first aid kit. They don't take up much room in your pack and even a simple kit can address most basic injuries. If you use something from your kit make sure to restock it so that it, and you, are always ready for whatever might occur.

Most cell phones have coverage in the Quarry. Because of this you should pack yours in the event that assistance is needed or to alert a medical provider that you are heading their way.

Standards

First Ascent Ethics:

This one section, found in just about every guidebook published, usually fuels debate. People's opinions differ, and standard, accepted practices vary from area to area. The guidelines and inclusions listed below are the consensus of local route developers and have been accepted to be the preferred criteria for establishing new routes in this area.

The Rock:

First off, let's dispel some rumors. The base rock of the Quarry is amazingly good, solid granite. The surface layer unfortunately has several loose flakes and blocks left as a byproduct of the past blasting activities. As such, a large part of establishing new routes involves the extensive cleaning of the potential new route. There are a few routes found in this guide that were clean to start with, but most are the result of many days of cleaning. If you are considering establishing a new route in the Quarry your first question to yourself should be whether or not you are willing to put in the time necessary to clean your proposed line. Most remaining lines are still covered with loose flakes and blocks that must be removed. Remember that this is predominantly a sport climbing area and that the end result of your first ascent efforts should be a safe and enjoyable route. If you are not willing to put in the cleaning time that the line requires, either look for a cleaner line or don't bother establishing a route.

Chipping and Gluing:

While both of these practices have been used to establish new routes at the Quarry, realize that the vast majority of the routes have no manufactured holds. Due to the extremely featured nature of the walls, there are usually other options than manufacturing a new hold.

Chipping has many definitions; from a little heavy-handed "creative cleaning" with the hammer or screwdriver, to all out drilling of pockets with a power drill. Realize that chipping as a rule is far from accepted and is at odds with local ethics at many climbing areas. Further, one must ask himself whether or not he is robbing future climbers by creating a hold where none currently exists. Climbing standards continue to rise with every passing season and what may seem improbable or even impossible today, may match the talents of tomorrow's climbers.

Gluing has been more readily accepted at the crag and is fairly prevalent. Due to the nature of the rock, extensive cleaning of all loose rock often leaves blank, scarred and very difficult lines where originally lines of features beckoned the first ascentionist. Gluing is discussed as a means of reinforcing either flexing holds or key holds that are suspect for future breakage. If you choose to use glue—accept the responsibility of doing it right and doing it neatly. A good glue job will not be readily obvious upon casual inspection of the reinforced hold. If you are thinking of using glue, please consult with someone who has experience in this matter and use the proper product. The most popular product is Sikadur AnchorFix-1, manufactured by Sika USA. It is a two-part structural epoxy that can be purchased at Home Depot and other locations. Its application is made using a regular, high strength caulking gun and requires clean, dry rock surfaces for proper adhesion. Once the epoxy has dried, file or sand any sharp edges and do your best to camouflage the glue to match the surrounding rock.

Standards

Leah Sandvoss on Nostalgia (11c) Photo: Andre Kiryanov

Standards

Anchors:

Due to the solid and dense nature of the Quarry granite, either sleeve or stud-type bolts can be used. Of these, the PowerBolt ("5-piece") by Powers-Rawl and the new Triplex bolt by Fixe are the preferred sleeve models due to their high strength ratings. If you choose to use stud-type bolts, the Fixe Wedge Bolts are the preferred choice. As in all areas, bolts made from stainless steel are preferred over those made from mild steel for their extended life span. In extremely solid rock, and on routes less than vertical, 3/8" x 2 1/4" bolts can be used. In all other situations 3/8" x 3" or 1/2" x 3" bolts should be considered the minimum bolt size. Due to the expanding nature of many of the Quarry flakes and cracks, a bolt is preferred and is much more reliable than a fixed piton.

Rappel bolting has been practiced on routes described in this guide. Whether you choose to place bolts on rappel or on lead—do a good job. Think about your bolt placements and make sure that they are in the best possible locations for clipping and for insuring that the rope runs cleanly and with minimal rope drag. Make sure that you place your bolts in solid sections of rock and that they tighten down correctly. If there is any doubt as to the integrity of a placed bolt it must be removed, the hole filled with epoxy, and camouflaged. The bolt can then be reinstalled in a location that allows for a sound installation.

As we are discussing the establishing of sport routes, lower off anchors are considerations as well. The minimum anchor system should be made up of chain and/or some sort of ring that would allow for the climbing rope to be passed through and the climber to rappel or be lowered off the route without having to leave anything behind. The best anchor available of this type is the Fixe Ring Anchor, and for multi-pitch climbs this is the preferred anchor system. For pitches of 30m/100' or less, an anchor made up of Fixe Ring Anchors is preferred over standard chain or screwlinks. These anchors are manufactured expressly for use as climbing anchors and offer a much higher strength rating than the anchor systems typically used and available at hardware or home improvement stores. They are also available in stainless steel, guaranteeing a long life span. Whatever style of anchor you choose to install make sure that it is made up of at least two points of connection to the rock and that it is installed in a location that allows for easy clipping by the climber and minimal wear on the rope.

Projects:

Because of the large investment of time, energy and money involved in establishing routes here, please respect other people's projects. Projects are generally labeled in one of two ways:

A green tag on the first bolt (or first bolt of a variation to an existing route) of a route means that the route has not been climbed, but that it has been "opened" by the route's equipper to be climbed by someone else. Feel free to attempt an open project such as this.

A red tag means that a route has not been climbed and that the route's equipper is still trying the route. Due to the large amount of cleaning work that goes into establishing a route in the Quarry, the route's difficulty may lie well within the equipper's abilities and the red tag signifies only that the work is not yet done on that particular route, not that the individual cannot climb the route and that you should. More than likely this means that the equipper has not yet finished cleaning

Standards

Matan Salmon on Metro (11a)

the route and that it might still be full of loose rock. Please respect the equipper's wishes and stay off of the route. Remember that a limited number of individuals have chosen to donate their time, energy and money to the development of new routes and that this is done ultimately to allow you more options at the crag. Show your appreciation and gratitude of this donation by staying off of the route until it has been climbed or changed to an open project.

Another possible explanation for a red tag on a route is to warn climbers of an unsafe condition on that route. Perhaps there is a dangerously loose hold, or one of the bolts and/or anchors are loose or worn and in need of replacement. If you see a red tag on a route that you know has been redpointed already this is more than likely the reason it's there. Once the condition has been corrected the tag will be removed.

Finally, remember that just about any piece of rock can be turned into a route. Before establishing a new route, ask yourself if your proposed line will be a valid addition to the area. Further, make sure that your line does not adversely impact or encroach on surrounding routes. If, after these considerations, you decide to establish your line – **DO A GOOD JOB!**

Standards

Difficulty Ratings:

The routes in the Quarry have been rated according to the Yosemite Decimal System. The 5th class prefix has been dropped for simplicity.

Although many of the routes described in this book are not new, it has only been recently that a broad consensus has been achieved in regards to the difficulty of the routes. As such, many of the ratings in this book may be different than what has previously been published. A huge effort was made to solicit the opinions of the local climbing community and several online databases were consulted as well. All of the feedback and information gathered was reviewed and resulted in the consensus ratings listed in this book. Your opinion may differ as all ratings are somewhat subjective. Because of this, it's generally best to treat all ratings as guidelines and not as absolutes.

That said, the following routes are considered benchmarks for their grade in the Quarry. While there are other routes with the same ratings that may feel easier or harder to you, these are the routes that were used as standards for the grade when rating comparisons were made.

Grade	Route	Grade	Route
10a	Industrial Bliss	12a	Raging Raptor
10b	Flexercise	12b	Torture Machine
10c	Trundle Trophy	12c	Graffiti Wisdom
10d	Tangerine Dream	12d	La Bella Donna
11a	Metro	13a	King Pin
11b	Flesh and Blood	13b	Enigma
11c	Nostalgia	13c	Gypsy
11d	Leviathan	13d	Temptation Supreme

Quality Ratings:

Quality ratings have been assigned based on the following factors: the amount of sustained climbing, the aesthetics of the moves, pump factor, exposure, location and rock quality. Squeeze jobs, contrived lines and poorly equipped routes subtract from the quality rating.

Generally, these quality ratings are intended only for comparison with other Quarry routes, and assume an acceptance of Quarry ethics (glue-reinforcement and some hold modification).

Rating	Meaning	Rating	Meaning
★★★★★	Area Classic	★★★	Very Good
★★★★	Excellent	★★	Good
★	Worth Doing	no stars	Poor

Following the quality rating an (r) indicates a runout route, an (x) indicates a very dangerous or deadly route.

Standards

Route Descriptions:

Following the name of the route, its difficulty and quality ratings are shown. Following this is a description of the gear that is required. First listed is the number of bolts found on the route, followed by any gear that might be required.

Pitch lengths are then noted. For example (30m/100') would mean that the pitch is 30 meters or 100 feet in length. Be sure to pay attention to this information and use the appropriate length of rope to ensure that you have enough length to lower back to the ground safely. Several Quarry routes are rope stretchers even with the use of a 60-meter rope. If there is any doubt that your rope is long enough, tie a knot in the ground end of the rope to prevent it from slipping through the belay device. There are also a handful of extended routes at the Quarry. These are routes that are longer than 100 feet (usually between 100 and 150 feet). The process for descending from the top of these routes is called L-P-L. Basically, the climber will lower from the topmost anchors to lower anchors at the 100 foot level and clip in. He will then pull the rope and lower to the ground from these anchors. When required, this will be noted in the route descriptions. Sometimes it is possible to lower safely without the L-P-L process by using a 70-meter rope. Where this is the case, that information will be given in the route description.

Next is a brief description of the route. If the route has multiple pitches this will be noted and each pitch will be described in ascending order.

Listed last is the first ascent information. FA signifies the person or persons involved in the first redpoint of the route. In the event of an aid climb that has been freed, FA will signify the person or persons involved in the first aid ascent, and FFA will signify the person or persons involved in the first free ascent of the route. OB signifies that the route has not yet been redpointed, but that the individual moves have been climbed by the person listed. EB signifies that the person listed equipped the route with its hardware, but has not climbed the individual moves.

Clean Aid Practices:

Many of the Quarry's aid routes follow seams, cracks and other natural features that accept standard free climbing protection. There are a few routes that may require some sections of nailing or copperheading, but the use of a hammer should always be secondary to the pursuit of clean climbing practices (where no hammer is used). This is especially true when aiding climbs that have gone free, as the use of hammer-placed protection will almost surely damage holds and impact the difficulty of the free climbing.

The Quarry is primarily considered a sport climbing area these days. As such, any efforts to practice aid climbing on established free climbs (whether sport or trad), must employ clean aid practices. If you feel the need to use a hammer and either pins or heads, please do so on one of the many features that have not been free climbed. There are also practice aid climbs found at the nearby Mount Rubidoux.

Standards

Equipment:

Almost exclusively the routes described in this guide are bolted sport routes. As such, nothing more than quickdraws and a rope are usually required. Bolt counts are given on all route descriptions, and the routes requiring gear list the type of gear required in their descriptions.

Some of the routes in this guide feature pitches longer than 80 feet in length. A 60 meter rope is required to lower off of, or to top-rope these routes. Please pay attention to route descriptions as they will provide the length of the pitch (i.e.: 30m/100'). Use this information as a guide when choosing the length of rope that you use on a given climb. Make sure that the rope you use is long enough to lower safely off the route's top anchors. It is highly suggested that a 60-meter rope be considered standard for climbing at the Quarry. Some routes require a 70-meter rope to safely lower. Where this is the case a warning is included in the route description.

It is also suggested that a rope bag or tarp be used for flaking out your rope at the base of the routes. Many of the base areas are dry and dusty and throwing your rope down in the dirt can cause tiny particles to work their way into the rope's inner core, possibly damaging the nylon strands found within. Further, a dust-coated rope will act as sandpaper on fixed anchors, severely decreasing their life span.

Betsy Dionne on Lovely Lady (10c)

Area History

Quarry Workers

Area History

General Area History

Many of the hills in the surrounding area have a rich deposit of limestone veins beneath their surfaces. The Riverside Cement Company (RCC) quarried several of the smaller hills in the early 1900's in order to access this limestone. The quarried stone was then crushed to a powdered form, creating the lime necessary for their cement mixture. So great was RCC's success in obtaining large quantities of lime from these smaller hills that they began looking at a much larger hill. Initial geological investigations showed that this hill also contained limestone, and around 1920 quarrying began on this larger hill.

The quarrying process was very labor intensive. Crews would drill vertical shafts at regular intervals from the top of the slope all the way down to ground level. Dynamite charges would then be placed into these shafts and timed blasts would be performed allowing multiple charges to detonate at once. This would cause a curtain of rock to fall away, exposing the layer of rock beneath. Once the limestone was salvaged from the fallen debris, the drilling crews would move back from the newly formed cliff edge and drill another series of shafts before repeating the process. As the blasting crews worked their way further and further into the hillside, the deposits of limestone became more scarce and then non-existent altogether. When this happened, RCC decided to abandon quarrying activity at this location and shifted their focus back to the smaller hillsides. There are still active lime quarries in the surrounding area, and several other abandoned quarries can be found as well.

To a large degree RCC's efforts at this location were a financial failure, but their failure was our windfall. The cliff line left behind when they halted their quarrying activities is what we now climb on. In fact, RCC reports that several of the workers involved with the quarrying operations had experience in rope work and basic climbing and rappelling techniques, and would often attempt to climb portions of the newly-exposed cliff towards the end of RCC's quarrying operations.

Area History

However, due to the blasted nature of the cliff, there was a large amount of loose rock and when more modern climbers first began exploring the area in the 1950's they found a huge cliff that most deemed too dangerous to climb. These climbers played on some of the more solid sections of rock, but interest soon died, and their focus shifted back to other regional crags that offered much more solid rock.

Sporadic climbing interest continued through the 1960's, but it was in the early 1970's that the next generation of talented local climbers, including Chris Robbins, began visiting the Quarry. Robbins began working on a steep arching crack on the right end of the formation. His success on *Agony Arch* (11b) resulted in one of the first 5.11's in Southern California and a subsequent flurry of Quarry activity by other local climbers. Most of this activity was centered on the right end, as once again climbers decided that the Quarry's main cliffs were too loose to climb safely. Robbins was a big proponent of Quarry climbing, and had he not died while climbing on El Capitan in 1978, I'm sure we would have seen much more development by him and his partners. As it was, interest in the Quarry somewhat died with Robbins, with the possible exception of Richard Jensen.

I'll be brief in describing Jensen's contributions to the Quarry, as Mark Smith has done an excellent job in summarizing the next era of Quarry climbing in the short essay immediately following this. However, it must be said that Jensen's commitment to the Quarry far surpassed that of any prior visitors. Jensen spent a fair amount of time in the Quarry in the late 1970's, continuing through the 1980's. He climbed with many different partners, but his partnership with Mark Smith is the one that is most remembered and most productive.

The two had dreams of climbing Yosemite Big Walls and felt that the Quarry was the perfect place to hone their skills. During the early 1980's Jensen and Smith, working together and individually, authored many of the more noteworthy Quarry aid climbs, and a handful of free climbs. The pair released the first guidebook to the area in 1982. This guide created a renewed interest, which was contagious, and before long climbers were looking at the Quarry as an aid climbing playground. Most climbers, however, still considered the main cliffs too loose to climb and stayed on the shorter and more solid sections of rock on the left and right ends of the cliff line.

Sporadic climbing activity continued, but the next real significant event occurred in 1992 when Mark Maynard visited the crag. Maynard thought that it was a shame to have such tall, steep walls seeing no action and decided that he would be the one to change things. He worked construction and had access to everything he thought that he would need. A few days later, Maynard pulled up to the base of the cliff with an industrial generator. Along with the generator Maynard brought a few hundred feet of cord and a demolition hammer (basically a small jackhammer). After drilling a bolt ladder up one particularly steep section of wall, he began to drill huge pockets. The resulting route was the first of its kind in Southern California, offering steep, gymnastic climbing on largely manufactured holds. As you can imagine, this did not go over well with the traditionally minded, aid climbing locals, and the route was chopped almost immediately.

Maynard's actions made other regional developers take notice of the area, and several of them came to check out the potential. It was obvious that the cliff was ideal as far as steepness and approach, but once again the area was dismissed as being too loose, too dangerous and requiring too much work to develop. Instead, those who visited remained primarily on the already developed climbs. Through the 1990's, the cliff continued to see climber visits, with a couple of new aid lines being added here and there, and a handful of the existing aid lines being freed.

Area History

All that changed in 2003. A local new route developer, Grahm Doe, was driving along the 60 freeway one afternoon in the ever-present southern California traffic. This traffic had him sitting at a standstill, with nothing to do but look around at the surrounding countryside and hills. That's when he first saw the Quarry. He immediately called his friend, Louie Anderson (another new route developer), to ask if he knew of the cliff. Anderson not only knew of the cliff, but had spent many years climbing there and dreaming of the possibilities, were the crag to be developed. The pair met the next day and walked back and forth along the base of the walls trying to gauge the potential of the area and to determine the amount of work that might be involved in establishing routes here. The amount of effort required seemed daunting, but knowing that they would not be alone in their efforts, they agreed to cautiously begin further development and reassess things as they went along. That day, they began rappelling down portions of the cliff, knocking off loose rock and drilling top rope anchors. After toproping these first lines they were sure that the crag was indeed worthy and made a commitment to cleaning things up and doing their best to turn the abandoned quarry into a local climbing resource.

The first area the pair focused on was the Taboo Area. Doe was interested in the tall runnel-lined face to the right, where he established *Rocky* (11d) and *Runaway* (12a), both named after the dog he rescued from the Quarry. Anderson was interested in trying to free a couple of aid climbs that he had first climbed years earlier. He was successful on both lines and the resulting routes, *Taboo* (12c) and *Forbidden Fruit* (12a) are brilliant. Doe's regular partner, Brent Webster began visiting the area as well and after adding other routes to the immediate area [including Doe's amazing climb, *The Saint* (13a), and Brent Webster's early addition, *Purple Haze* (12b), the group started to branch out, adding selected routes scattered along the length of the cliff. Most of the more obvious lines at the cliff were bolted first and these have become some of the classics at the crag.

Over the next two years, over 100 routes were bolted (radiating out from the developed routes on the different walls). Many of the remaining aid routes were freed and the majority of the ¼" bolts on the old free climbs were replaced with larger, stronger bolts. Along with Anderson, Doe, and Webster, Gary Henning and Matt Callender lent a hand in the massive amount of work required to clean up the routes, the base areas and to build the initial climbers' trails around the base of the cliff. Everyone involved was amazed at the overall quality of the climbing; it being far better than any of them imagined that it would be. They began to invite others to come and sample the routes and as those climbers enjoyed themselves, they invited others.

An updated edition of the guidebook was authored by Anderson in 2005. This book offered information on approximately 160 free climbs and the majority of the known aid climbs. Many climbers in the region had driven by the area, and some had climbed there, but few really appreciated the quantity and quality of the climbing that was offered by the Quarry. Development did not stop with the release of that guidebook. Unfortunately Doe moved out of the area shortly after its release, but the others remained focused on adding new routes to the cliff. In addition, Tony Sartin and Bill Leventhal became interested in the potential of the area and began to visit more regularly.

In an attempt to attract others to the crag, Anderson gave away the first ascent of a few of his harder projects prior to his own redpoints. *Weapons of Mass Destruction* (13a), redpointed by Alan Moore, and *Mission Possible* (13c) and *Temptation Supreme* (13d), both redpointed by Chris Lindner are the best examples of this. All three should be on any high-level climber's tick list.

Area History

Henning became very interested in the large expanse of rock at the right end of the cliff line. There had been sporadic climbing activity there over the years, but this huge section of cliff remained largely undeveloped. The area became known as The Alcove and Henning added several quality lines there, with most of them extending all the way to the top of the cliff. This area has the highest concentration of long pitches at the crag and is the last of the main cliff line areas to go into the sun, due to the slightly concave shape of the crag. Both of those traits made his additions instantly popular.

Once the majority of the new lines in The Alcove had been climbed, Henning began to notice small sections of steep rock interspersed among the lower-angled sections of rock in the Slab City area, at the opposite end of the crag. He made the judgment that since the area was a manmade cliff (due to the prior blasting and quarrying operations), that it would be acceptable to manufacture holds on a larger scale than what had been done previously in the Quarry. He began to systematically add new routes in that area, the majority of which climbed very steep terrain on primarily positive holds. The resulting routes are very powerful and offer a style of climbing not found elsewhere in the area. His routes *S.F.R.* (12b) and *Love Nest* (12d) are the best of those new routes.

Chris Miller, Euan Cameron, and Craig Britton became interested in a few moderate lines at the cliff and added routes in the Slab City area. In an attempt to create an option for entry-level climbers, this group and Anderson also bolted a new area at the far right end of the crag that was called Schoolhouse Rock. This area offers the highest concentration of easier routes in the Quarry and has become quite popular with new leaders.

During the time between the last guidebook and this new edition, Anderson has continued to add new routes. He also revisited some of the first areas developed and performed sometimes massive cleaning projects in an attempt to remove the more dangerous sections of loose rock. In some cases this led to routes changing severely in difficulty, and in a few cases being more or less erased altogether. An entirely new area, The Fun Factory, was developed near the Agony Arch area. The intent in developing this area was to provide a collection of easier and shorter climbs than those found elsewhere at the Crag. The hope was that this area would be less intimidating for newer leaders and less experienced climbers. In the last months preceding the release of this book, Anderson bolted the remaining lines that had been on his radar; including the airy roof climb *Exposure* (12b) and the instantly popular *The Ultimate* (12d).

This guidebook represents the current stage of development. There are still a handful of potential routes to be climbed, and no doubt many of them will be climbed in the years to come. The area is largely developed though and future additions will be limited. The area has quickly become the premier sport climbing crag in southern California; a recognition that it more than deserves. It's likely that the future of the area will involve less new route development, and that the focus will shift instead to area maintenance, ongoing cleanup efforts and continued positive relations with the land owners and neighboring residents.

Area History

Louie Anderson on Taboo (12c) *Photo: Perri Nguyen*

Area History

Early Climbing History of the Riverside Quarry

The unusual history of rock climbing at the Riverside Quarry derives from the cliff's unique and explosive genesis. During the first half of the twentieth century, the Riverside Cement Company mined what is now the Riverside Quarry by exploding successive layers of the cliff face with copious amounts of dynamite. The massive explosions necessary to blast apart the high-quality rock led to the steep walls and crisp edges that make the Quarry of today a sport climber's dream. However, those earth-shattering explosions also created a huge amount of loose rock and unstable blocks, many of which clung precariously to the cliff. Thanks to years of painstaking work, most of the loose rock has been cleared via rappel, effectively "de-paving" the way to the modern sport climbs now enjoyed on the Quarry's various walls. In all likelihood, those new to the cliff probably cannot appreciate how dangerous and dominating the Quarry once appeared.

Sadly, the Quarry's earliest climbing history went undocumented. That history can only be inferred from the scant evidence of a few scattered artifacts. Initial activity appears to have begun at the Quarry's left margin, where the cliff is shorter and somewhat less shattered. Two or three soft iron pitons – a trademark of the pre-70's rack – found on *Gulp Swallow* suggest that its first ascent probably predates 1970. In the same area, *Romp* along with *Vertical Vee*, a surprisingly difficult aid (now free) route, saw their first pitches established sometime prior to 1980.

In the 60's or early 70's, an endeavor to reach the rim of the Quarry's main cliff ended a short pitch and halfway up what later became *Stay of Execution*. Also, in the region between the Shield and Taboo areas, a three-piton belay/rappel station was observed, along with a stray piton lower down. These features indicate that the cliff was probably attempted at that point as well, although the belay station might merely mark the midpoint of a rappel from the rim. The complete lack of evidence of climbing activity on the upper half of the main cliff suggests that no team completed a base-to-rim ascent.

Chris Robbins put the Quarry onto So Cal's climbing radar screen in the mid-70's when he went to work on the classic *Agony Arch* and the then unnamed, one-bolt face climb *Valiant Flail* to *No Avail*. Tragically, Chris perished in a climbing accident on El Capitan in 1978. The exact accomplishments of Chris and his friends are foggy, but the first ascent of *Agony Arch* is generally attributed to Robbins. Perhaps some of those from that era will come forward with more details. What is certain is that the Quarry was now on the map.

The opening of the Agony Arch Area hardly ushered in a new wave of development. The cliff was often gritty and the aesthetics of the base less than appealing – not to mention the fact that loose blocks and flakes, ranging in size from "golf balls" to "refrigerators," clung to nearly every potential new route. Southern California climbing ethics of that era valued ground-up ascents; as such, inspecting or cleaning routes on rappel was frowned on, to say the least. Since top-down prepping of climbs was not practiced, many local climbers regarded the Quarry as a death trap to be avoided. That view dominated Quarry activity throughout the 70's and much of the 80's, greatly hindering the development of new routes.

In the late 70's, Richard Jensen relocated to Riverside not far from the Quarry. As a 19-year old, Richard began exploring several abandoned quarries in the Riverside area. The cliff now known as the Riverside Quarry proved to be his most intriguing discovery. Finding climbing partners for the Quarry became a serious challenge as the cliff was vaguely known and had a reputation

Area History

Richard Jensen on first ascent of Reign of Pain

for being loose and dangerous. Keeping partners was a challenge as well since most of its early routes were first ascent aid climbs which required a lot of hard work to establish. Through a number of partners, Jensen launched the real genesis of serious Quarry development, which began in 1979, and continued through the spring of 1981. This time frame saw complete ascents of *Vertical Vee* and *Romp*, as well as the establishment of *Feetal Rearrangement* and *Unexpected Difficulties*.

Richard introduced me to the Quarry in the spring of 1981. He led a fairly easy pitch and brought me up to an exposed belay shelf. Little did I discern that his main objective in dragging me to this unfamiliar cliff was to size me up as a potential Quarry climbing partner. I unwittingly agreed when Richard slyly suggested I take the next lead. As I traversed out from the anchor, I noticed a couple of spots to set protection. I bypassed these, figuring that I'd rather not punctuate a spectacular fall by being brained from a shower of falling rock dislodged from ripped placements. As fate would have it, my primary handhold came off about thirty feet into the lead. All efforts to maintain a calm and cool façade dissolved as I tried to manage a growing panic. Fortunately the climbing was only 5.7, or so I was told, and the crisis soon passed. "Why would *anyone* climb here?" I mused. Yet something drew me in. Was it the privacy and isolation of the cliff; the need to push beyond my own prior experiences; the innate need to explore? Perhaps all of these reasons compelled my return.

Development of the Quarry's cliffs differed from that of most other locations. Usually the pioneers in a new area climb one or more routes to get a feel for the rock, and then start putting up new climbs, each of which is fundamentally similar to others

Climber's Guide: Riverside Quarry • 43

Area History

Richard Jensen at the mid belay on first ascent of Reign of Pain

in the area. While each climb has its unique qualities and its own rating, outcomes of new climbs are normally somewhat predictable beforehand. This paradigm didn't fit the Quarry. For example, on one occasion we set up an anchor comprised entirely of pitons. When we jugged back up to the anchor the next day, one of the pins was loose and another removable by hand! Disconcerting events such as this left us uncertain as to the boundaries of what we could sanely attempt. Was it reasonable to nail the side of a block that might dislodge? What about nailing under such a block and then along its side as well? At what point did a large block simply become the cliff itself, so large that you didn't worry about dropping it? Lots of obvious lines could be attempted, but which if any of these *should* be attempted? Since some amount of rock was dislodged on nearly every first ascent, few first ascents were routine; few outcomes were predictable. Consequently, we limited our activity to the extreme left and right margins of the Quarry, avoiding the looser, steeper, and obviously more perilous main wall altogether.

The completion of *Stay of Execution* in the fall of 1981 marked the start of the Quarry's great leap forward. Everyone, Richard included, had considered the entire expanse of wall to the right of the Slab City area to be unsuitable for climbing. One day Richard had the wild, hare-brained "vision" to suggest we amble up to the base of the big roof that dominates the center of the Quarry. Today, the thought of walking the cliff to scope routes may seem trivial, but at the same time the notion of climbing the main cliff was universally regarded as insane. We spied an old attempt to reach the roof that ended about eighty feet up. We decided to give it a go. Eventually we passed the previous high point and gained the back recess of the Great Roof on what would eventually be dubbed *Stay of Execution*. The obvious exit from the recess of the roof followed a traverse out its right side, a crack stuffed with loose rock that culminated in a block so wild as to deserve mention in *Ripley's Believe It Or Not*. The narrow point of this two-foot long spike was cammed into the crack, with the rest of the projectile jutting straight out. How could this menacing block have possibly been formed from any explosion? Richard led out to it, trying without success to gingerly dislodge it. It seemed that the only way to clear the 50+ pound horror was with a stick of dynamite, or by taking it on with alligator wrestling techniques. We tucked our collective tails between our legs and reluctantly retreated. Defeated by the Great Roof, we couldn't shake the climb from our minds. A few weeks later we returned for an epic rematch. Armed with only a crag

Area History

Louie Anderson and Richard Jensen on Fowl Play Circa 1983

hammer, saucer-eyed Richard finally dislodged the spike, sending it on a free fall to the talus below. The next day the Roof Area had its first route. With the seemingly insurmountable Great Roof conquered without loss of life, the floodgates opened for more daunting routes.

In 1982, a set of topos and descriptions were compiled and published as *The Climber's Guide to the Riverside Quarry*. Over time, a sequence of increasingly difficult ascents appeared: *Pursuit of Pain* (A4), *Reign of Pain* (A4 loose), *Terms of Forever* (A4+), and *Bird of Prey* (A5); the latter three each giving way to the next hardest aid route south of Yosemite. Through the guidebook and word of mouth, more parties were arriving to check things out. Seeing other climbers scaling the Quarry's cliffs was no longer an unusual sight, although the dangers of loose rock combined with a ground-up ethic continued to minimize the development of new routes.

Bird of Prey (1987) marked the end of the Golden Age of the Quarry's development. Those who had been instrumental in transforming this unique cliff into a legitimate climbing area eventually moved on to other endeavors. The Quarry of old was destined to be swept up into the sport climbing wave of the 1990's. Slowly, many if not most of the great original routes gave way to this trend. At present, *Bird of Prey* and a number of other hard aid routes no longer exist, having been literally peeled off via rappel and overtaken by sport climbs. Other aid routes now go free. Some free and formerly aid climbs have had additional bolts added on rappel to bring them more in line with the current sport climbing nature of the cliff. Nonetheless, some routes such as *Pursuit of Pain* remain as an example of the Quarry's earlier years.

Area History

Often times it is hard to understand, let alone encapsulate for others, exactly what makes an object "special." In reflecting back on the "glory days" of the Quarry, I struggle to understand why this blocky cliff, once so ignored, captivated my imagination. In the 1980's, abundant first ascent opportunities existed across California in almost every direction. The Quarry's intrigue, therefore, could not derive merely from its abundance of virgin rock. Rather, it derived from the search for the then unknown limits of what could and couldn't be climbed, an exploration made necessary by the cliff's unique nature. The experience of that exploration, I believe, made the Quarry's early development so intriguing, meaningful, and rewarding.

The Quarry of today has come of age as an amazing sport climbing venue. Still, it wasn't that long ago that the Quarry was a private place of seemingly unlimited opportunity for those who wanted an experience found nowhere else south of the Sierras. The type of adventure now found only on more remote cliffs was once part and parcel of the Quarry, a magical place just a few minutes' drive down the Pomona Freeway.

Mark Smith
October 5, 2008

Photos from the Mark Smith Collection

Mark Smith at the belay on Pursuit of Pain

Developer Profiles

While Louie Anderson remains the driving force behind Quarry climbing and upkeep, the Quarry's popularity and climbing options are the results of others' efforts as well. Three climbers in particular deserve recognition for their hard work and for the routes they brought to all of us:

Grahm Doe on Gypsy (13c)

Grahm Doe

Grahm is largely responsibility for re-motivating Louie Anderson on developing the Quarry. The two shared the initial vision for what the area could become and for the first few years of activity, Grahm was every bit as active as anyone else and would routinely walk the cliff line looking for his next project. Often times, he would approach a blank expanse of wall and pick the one line that called to him. Once he succeeded on that route, he would jump to an entirely different section of the Quarry. As a result, he has high-quality routes scattered across the length on the cliff band.

His better routes include: *Rocky* (11d), *Torture Machine* (12b), *Balrog* (12b), *Microquarry* (12c), *The Saint* (13a), and *Gumption* (13c). However, he is probably best known for a route that he actually did not redpoint – *Gypsy* (13c).

As he was known to do, Grahm approached the then undeveloped wall and immediately decided to attack the line of strength that eventually became Gypsy. He bolted the line and over the course of a year or so worked on it without a redpoint, methodically deciphering the devious technical cruxes of this Quarry test piece. When he and his wife made the decision to move out of the area, the pressure to send intensified and Grahm was on the route right up to the day prior to moving, coming ever so close, but ultimately having to leave without the redpoint. His friends, Brent Webster and Louie Anderson did the first and second ascents of this great route, but it will always be looked at as Grahm's route.

Grahm has since moved to a small mountain town outside of Yosemite Valley, where he continues to explore and develop new climbing options, primarily in the Shuteye Ridge area.

Developer Profiles

Brent Webster high on Sky Pilot (12c)

Brent Webster

Brent has an infectious psyche and motivation for climbing. That positive and optimistic approach to development kept morale high during the first years of continued development at the crag. Those days were often filled with hours of cleaning and bolting, where the majority of the day was spent hanging in a harness and wrestling with loose features. Brent's jokes and sometimes childlike enthusiasm somehow made those days far less daunting than they could have been.

Those who've climbed with Brent will agree that when watching him climb, it appears as though he doesn't get pumped. He can either do the move or not, but seldom does he fail due to a lack of endurance. Instead, Brent's redpoint efforts are more about the process of dissecting the climb and figuring the moves and then executing them well, than seemingly having to deal with any real fitness deficit at all. He just goes and goes…

Brent was not as prolific in his new route activity as some others, but he was a big support player in the efforts of all of the other major developers. Primarily partnering with Grahm Doe and Gary Henning, he was more often than not the one on the other end of their ropes. That's not to say that he didn't establish some good routes of his own though. The best of Brent's routes include: *Schwazzle Dazzle* (11c), *Silver Streaker* (12a), *Anger Management* (12b), *Trepanation* (12c), *and Choss Goggles* (12c). He also spent a fair amount of time cleaning the steep, *tall wall* in the *Slide Zone* and had the original vision for that wall's open project route, *Mud Monster* (14b/c).

Developer Profiles

Gary Henning

Gary Henning on Burly Boogie (13a)

Gary became involved in the new phase of development at the Quarry not too long after the other players. In the beginning, he was happy just to climb the other routes and offer his support. However, once he saw the continued quality of the emerging routes, he threw his drill into the mix as well.

Gary has a select few routes here and there along the cliff line, but is known more for his developments at either end of the crag. Prior to Gary's involvement, there was not a lot of attention given to the tall faces at the right end of the cliff. Gary was drawn to these walls and most of his initial efforts were made on what was to become known as The Alcove. He produced many fine routes there, and spent quite a bit of time in making the base areas as flat and comfortable as possible.

Gary's next focus was at the opposite end of the crag in the Slab City area. There are many bulges, roofs and shorter sections of steep rock in that area, and most of the existing routes climbed around and in between them. Gary decided that it was a shame to not be able to enjoy those steeper sections of rock. The only problem was that most of them were completely devoid of climbable features. Never one to go with the flow, Gary decided that given the fact that the entire cliff was the result of explosive charges and quarrying, that a continuation of those man-made efforts was in order. He proceeded to manufacture many powerful routes on those steeper sections of rock. Not everyone was happy to see this happen, but no one could argue that the resulting routes were fun. Nor could the style of climbing experienced on those routes be found elsewhere in the Quarry.

The standouts of Gary's routes include: *Magic Mushroom* (11b), *Salubrious* (11c), *S.F.R.* (12b), *Love Nest* (12d), *La Bella Donna* (12d), and *Hands of Time* (13a).

Area Overview

Area	Page
A. Slab City	**52**
B. Metro Sector	**69**
C. Left of the Roof	**72**
D. Roof Area	**83**
E. Right of the Roof	**98**
F. Torture Machine Area	**104**
G. Slander Sector	**110**
H. Rubble Row	**113**

Area Overview

Area	Page
I. Slide Zone	120
J. The Tall Wall	124
K. The Shield	126
L. Anger Management Area	133
M. Taboo Area	138
N. The Alcove	153
O. Schoolhouse Rock	158
P. The Fun Factory	162
Q. Agony Arch Area	168

Slab City

Slab City

Slab City

Located at the far left end of the formation, Slab City offers convenient climbing due to its ground level base. This area features one of the highest concentrations of easier sport climbing found at the crag, with the standouts being *White Light* (5.7), *Feetal Rearrangement* (5.8), *Groove Factor* (5.9), *and Mantle Marathon* (10a). The area also offers some of the best crack climbs on the cliff, including *Gulp Swallow* (10c), *Vertical Vee* (11d), *Romp Direct* (12a), *and Punish the Puppy* (12b). A couple of harder, technical sport climbs will challenge the stronger climbers, with standouts being *Microquarry* (12c) *and Synergy* (12d). Finally, the addition of several manufactured routes on the area's many steep bulges offers powerful and bouldery sections of climbing on steep terrain, not found elsewhere in the Quarry.

Slab City

Slab City Left

1. Diagonal Direct 11a ★
2. Hoochie Mama 11a ★★
3. Cling Thing 10d ★★
4. Hang Thang 11a ★★
5. Whiplash 12b ★★
6. Peter Principle 11c ★★
7. Pigeon, the Other White Meat 10c ★
8. Shattered Dreams 10c ★★
9. Unexpected Difficulties 11a ★★, 11b ★
10. Walk the Plank 11a ★★
11. Pandora's Box 11c ★★
12. S.F.R. 12b ★★★
13. Punish the Puppy 12b ★★★★
14. Tyranny 12b ★★
15. Jeep Jockey 12c ★★
16. The Enforcer 12c ★★
17. Marathon Man 11b ★
18. Mantle Marathon 10a ★★
19. Mantlepiece 10c ★★
20. Bottom Feeder 11b ★
21. Goody Two Shoes 10b ★★
22. Feetal Rearrangement 5.8 ★★, 10c ★, A2 ★
23. Chas' Route 11c ★
24. The Fine Line 10d ★★
25. Pucker Power 12b (r) ★★★
26. Sendsual Feeling 12a ★★

Slab City

Routes are described from left to right.

❶ Diagonal Direct 11a ★ ❏

8 Bolts to a double ring anchor, 21m/70'. Begin climbing at a lieback block, halfway between to the two embedded metal quarry rods. Climb straight over a bulge, before traversing right to join *Hoochie Mama* at its fourth bolt. Finish on that route. FA: Louie Anderson 2007

❷ Hoochie Mama 11a ★★ ❏

7 Bolts to a double ring anchor, 18m/60'. Starts ten feet right of *Diagonal Direct* and three feet right of the right metal rod. Climbs over a blocky bulge, following shattered seams, and finishes through the steep bulge above on lieback flakes. You may want to use a long draw on the fourth bolt (or skip it) to reduce rope drag. FA: Louie Anderson 2007

❸ Cling Thing 10d ★★ ❏

7 bolts to a double ring anchor, 18m/60'. Begins at a chest high hole in the rock and climbs past a sloping ledge and over a shallow bulge, before climbing up and right to a corner. Climb the lieback flake to anchors on the block above. FA: Louie Anderson 2007.

❹ Hang Thang 11a ★★ ❏

8 bolts to a double ring anchor, 18m/60'. Start climbing eight feet right of *Cling Thing* at a heavily graffitied section. Climbs up to and through a bulge, just left of a gold streak, before moving left to join *Cling Thing* at its fourth bolt. Finish on that route. FA: Louie Anderson 2007.

❺ Whiplash 12b ★★ ❏

8 bolts to a double ring anchor, 18m/60'. Begins on the left side of the arête and climbs past a few shallow ledges, continuing up the arête above. Ultimately finishes up the short slab section before the anchors. FA: Louie Anderson 2007.

❻ Peter Principle 11c ★★ ❏

7 bolts to a double ring anchor, 18m/60'. Starts on the right side of the arête and climbs the center of a shattered face, up to and over a shallow roof. Finishes at the anchors of *Whiplash*. FA: Louie Anderson 2007.

❼ Pigeon, the Other White Meat 10c ★ ❏

6 bolts to a double ring anchor, 18m/60'. A link up. Clip the first two bolts of *Shattered Dreams*, before moving up and left and clipping two independent bolts. Joins *Peter Principle* and clips the last two bolts of that route. Awkward climbing that is a little harder than it appears. FA: Chris Miller, Euan Cameron 10-2007.

❽ Shattered Dreams 10c ★★ ❏

7 bolts to a double ring anchor, 18m/60'. Climbs the obvious, shattered crack system, up the center of the face. There is a height-dependant crux just before the anchors. FA: Louie Anderson 2007

Slab City

⑨ Unexpected Difficulties 11a ★★ ❏, 11b ★ ❏

Pitch One: 7 Bolts and nuts and cams to 2 ½" to a sling belay, 27m/90'. Climb the shattered and jagged hand and fist crack before traversing right on a thin crack below the roof. Ends at the double ring anchor of *Pandora's Box*. Pitch Two: Some ¼" bolts, nuts and cams from tiny to 1 ½" to a double chain anchor, 18m/60'. From the anchor, traverse up and right through a small notch and follow the thin seam above the ledges to the top of the slab. FA: Richard Jensen, Dean Woods 1981. FFA: Richard Jensen, Mark Smith 3-1982.

⑩ Walk the Plank 11a ★★ ❏

8 Bolts and nuts and cams to 2 ½" to a gear anchor, 42m/140'. A variation. Start as for *Unexpected Difficulties*, but continue traversing past the double ring anchor onto a large, flat ledge. Belay at the right end of the ledge. Finish up the final pitch of *Feetal Rearrangement* or on *The Fine Line*. FA: Richard Jensen, Mark Smith 3-1982.

⑪ Pandora's Box 11c ★★ ❏

9 bolts to a double ring anchor, 24m/80'. Begin climbing on the right side of the left of two blocky boulders, just to the right of *Shattered Dreams*. Clip two bolts and then continue past the ledge above. Traverse up and right into a right-facing dihedral feature. Continues up a lieback flake and then up the exposed, shallow arête above. Slopey climbing and technical moves give this route a nice challenge at the finish. FA: Louie Anderson 2007.

⑫ S.F.R. 12b ★★★ ❏

11 bolts to a double ring anchor, 24m/80'. This route starts off the top of the right boulder. Pre-clip the first bolt (in the roof). Pull over the low roof and continue up the face above to reach the horizontal crack system blow the upper roof. Climb through this roof and follow the right-leaning, hanging arête on manufactured holds. FA: Gary Henning 2010.

⑬ Punish the Puppy 12b ★★★★ ❏

9 bolts to a double ring anchor, 24m/80'. The original Richard Jensen route has suffered a large amount of rock fall over the years. The remaining line has been further cleaned of loose rock, bolted and realigned to provide this new challenging route. Climb up a thin seam located in the narrow corridor behind the large, ground-level boulder. Follow the obvious crack system above as it winds around a bulging section of rock. When you reach the roof, traverse left along a horizontal crack to the crux lip encounter. This powerful and exposed sequence leads you up the short headwall crack to the shared anchors with *Pandora's Box*. This climb is slightly easier now due to the manufactured holds on *S.F.R.* that can be used for this route. FA: (original line and finish): Richard Jensen 1982. FA: (current version) Louie Anderson 2007.

⑭ Tyranny 12b ★★ ❏

6 bolts to 2 open shuts, 18m/60'. Climb the vertical face on crimps and edges, starting four feet right of *Punish the Puppy*. Continue past a dished section through the roof above. FA: Louie Anderson 2003.

Slab City

Valarie Heredia on Lovely Lady (10c)

⓯ Jeep Jockey 12c ★★ ❏

7 bolts to 2 open shuts, 18m/60'. A link-up. Climb *The Enforcer* to its 3rd bolt before traversing left and joining *Tyranny* at its 3rd bolt. This route climbs the best (and hardest) sections of both routes. FA: Louie Anderson 2003.

⓰ The Enforcer 12c ★★ ❏

10 bolts to 2 open shuts, 24m/80'. A hard boulder problem at the start leads to much easier climbing and a funky roof sequence. This route used to end at the ledge above the first roof, but has now been extended through the steep headwall above the ledge on manufactured holds. FA(original route): Louie Anderson 2003. FA (with extension): Gary Henning 2010.

⓱ Marathon Man 11b ★ ❏

7 bolts to a double ring anchor, 21m/70'. Start climbing from the top of a small pile of rocks at the base of the wall, six feet right of *The Enforcer*. After clipping the high first bolt, balancy and powerful arête moves lead to a no-hands rest at a ledge above. Continue climbing the face above to the right of a large, perched block. Move through the roof above to finish at shared anchors with *Mantle Marathon*. FA: Euan Cameron, Chris Miller 2007

⓲ Mantle Marathon 10a ★★ ❏

8 bolts to a double ring anchor, 21m/70'. Begin climbing seven feet right of *Marathon Man* and ten feet left of the blunt arête. Follow the line of a very thin seam as it passes several small ledges. FA: Louie Anderson 2003.

Slab City

⑲ Mantlepiece 10c ★★ ❏
7 or 8 bolts to a double ring anchor, 21m/70'. Start six feet right of *Mantle Marathon*. Climb up and right to a small overlap and a somewhat reachy move to a large, flat edge. Mantle onto the short ramp, having clipped three independent bolts, where you can either move left to clip the fourth bolt of *Mantle Marathon* and finish on that route or move up and right to the fourth bolt of *Bottom Feeder* and finish on that route. FA: Euan Cameron, Chris Miller 2007.

⑳ Bottom Feeder 11b ★ ❏
7 bolts to a double ring anchor, 21m/70'. Start just right of the arête and climb up the shallow dihedral system passing some white rock. Continue up the slabs above staying more or less on the arête. FA: Louie Anderson 2003.

㉑ Goody Two Shoes 10b ★★ ❏
7 bolts to a double ring anchor, 18m/60'. This route starts 12 feet right of *Bottom Feeder* and climbs straight up the center of the slab. FA: Louie Anderson 2003.

㉒ Feetal Rearrangement 5.8 ★★ ❏, 10c ★ ❏, A2 ★ ❏
Pitch One: 8 bolts to a double ring anchor, 21m/70'. Begin climbing at the right side of the slab, where the rock turns white. After clipping the second bolt traverse up and left to the top of the slab. Pitch Two: Nuts and cams to 3" to a gear anchor, 11m/35'. From the anchors traverse left passing another set of rings and climb through the roof via a steep crack system. Belay over the lip. Pitch Three: Thin pins, nuts and cams from tiny to 1" to a bolted anchor, 18m/60'. Continue up the thin seam to the top of the slab. Could go free with some cleaning. FA: Richard Jensen, Dean Woods 1980.

㉓ Chas' Route 11c ★ ❏
2 bolts (one requiring a rivet hanger or wired nut) to a double ring anchor, 8m/25'. From the first pitch anchors of *Feetal Rearrangement*, climb out the steep right wall, clipping one old ¼" bolt (with a hanger) and one without a hanger. Finishes at the bolted anchor on the ledge above and right of this short face. FA: Mark Smith, Richard Jensen 6-1981. FFA: Chas Wilson 2007

㉔ The Fine Line 10d ★★ ❏
Some bolts, RURPS, blades, small nuts and cams to a double ring anchor, 27m/90'. From a belay just above *Feetal Rearrangement's* roof, traverse right following a very thin horizontal seam. When the seam ends merge and finish up the second pitch crack of *Vertical Vee*. FA: Richard Jensen, Mark Smith 7-1981. FFA: Same party 3-1982.

㉕ Pucker Power 12b (r) ★★★ ❏
12 bolts to 2 open shuts, 30m/100'. Start as for *Feetal Rearrangement*, but after clipping the second bolt climb straight up through some blocky roofs. Traverse left under the steep arête before crossing it at mid-height and climbing through a bulge (via a hidden crimp) to a ledge. From the ledge climb the smooth upper slab (passing a bolted anchor), following the diagonal seam. Due to the friable nature of the upper seam, it has been bolted. To protect the route as a free climb, it should no longer be aided. FA: From top of *Feetal Rearrangement* through right bulge and up the upper seam (on aid) by Mark Smith, Richard Jensen 6-1981. New direct start and FFA of upper seam by Louie Anderson 2004.

Madison Anderson on Feetal Rearrangement (5.8)

Slab City

Slab City Center

- ㉗ **Microquarry 12c** ★★★
- ㉘ **Flawed Perfection 12c** ★★★
- ㉙ **Synergy 12d** ★★★
- ㉚ **Vertical Vee 11d** ★★★
- ㉛ **Flying Vee 11d** ★★★
- ㉜ **Approach Pitch 5.7**
- ㉝ **Grandma Seizure 11b** ★
- ㉞ **Romp 10c** ★★★
- ㉟ **New Directions 12a** ★★★
- ㊱ **Romper Room 12b** ★★
- ㊲ **Romp Direct 12a** ★★★
- ㊳ **F.U.B.A.R. 12b** ★★
- ㊴ **All Tapped Out 12d** ★★
- ㊵ **Love Nest 12d** ★★★
- ㊶ **Bottoms Up 12c** ★★
- ㊷ **Gulp Swallow 10c** ★★★
- ㊸ **Chaste, but Tasty 12a** ★★
- ㊹ **Lovely Lady 10c** ★★★★

Slab City

㉖ Sendsual Feeling 12a ★★ ❏

14 bolts to a double ring anchor, 30m/100'. Begin climbing ten feet right of *Pucker Power*, just right of the arête. Climb the smooth face past two bolts and continue through the blocky terrain above, to ultimately finish up the smooth slab. FA: Gary Henning 2010.

㉗ Microquarry 12c ★★★ ❏

13 bolts to 2 open shuts, 30m/100'. Climb the steep dihedral ten feet right of *Feetal Rearrangement* and continue through the bulge above. Finishes up the polished upper slab on tiny holds and balancey moves. FA: Grahm Doe 2003.

㉘ Flawed Perfection 12c ★★★ ❏

16 bolts to a double biner anchor, 30m/100'. This route starts just right of *Microquarry*. Climb the right side of stair-stepped, blocky features. Continue up the short arête above a shallow bulge, and then up the clean face above. Finishes up the smooth slab. FA: Gary Henning 2009.

㉙ Synergy 12d ★★★ ❏

13 bolts to 2 open shuts, 30m/100'. 8 feet right of *Microquarry* is a small recess. Stem up this and climb the right-facing corner system. Climb over a small bulge and finish by following a seam on the slab above. FA: Louie Anderson 2004.

㉚ Vertical Vee 11d ★★★ ❏, 5.8 ❏

Pitch One: 7 bolts to a double ring anchor, 19m/65'. Scramble up the initial, short face and climb the left-facing corner system just right of *Synergy*, using thin seams in a pair of shallow dihedrals. At mid-height cross over to the right seam. Pitch Two: Nuts and cams to 3" to a double ring anchor, 12m/40'. Stem out the alcove and follow the broken crack system above. FA (first pitch): Unknown, but prior to 1980. FA (entire route): Richard Jensen, Don Woods, Dean Woods 1980. FFA (first pitch – on gear): Louie Anderson 2004. Bolts by Bill Leventhal (with permission) 2006.

㉛ Flying Vee 11d ★★★ ❏

8 bolts to a double ring anchor, 21m/70'. A variation finish to the regular *Vertical Vee* route. When nearing the end of that route, move right onto the face and finish up the slab above. FA: Bill Leventhal 2006

㉜ Approach Pitch 5.7 ❏

5 bolts to a double ring anchor, 17m/45'. From the anchors of *Flying Vee,* climb up and left to gain a break in the slab. Follow this up and right to anchors below the hanging summit block above. This route is used to approach *Grandma Seizure*. FA: Bill Leventhal 2006

㉝ Grandma Seizure 11b ★ ❏

4 bolts to a double ring anchor, 11m/35'. Climb up to a high first bolt and then follow the obvious flake left through the bulge. When you reach the ledge at the end of the flake, climb the left face on cruxy crimps, passing one bolt. This steep line could be pretty good with some more cleaning. FA: Bill Leventhal 2006

Slab City

㉞ Romp 10c ★★★ ❏

Bolts, nuts and cams to 1 ½", including micro cams, to a 2-bolt belay, **36m/120'**. Start 8 feet right of *Vertical Vee* and climb up to the underside of the big block. Traverse up and right following a diagonal crack system, and continue traversing under the roof to anchors at the far right end of the roof. Originally led on gear, this route now has some bolts due to the addition of adjacent sport climbs. FA: Richard Jensen 1980. FFA: Richard Jensen, Mark Smith 1982.

㉟ New Directions 12a ★★★ ❏

13 bolts to a double ring anchor, 29m/95'. Begin climbing eight feet right of *Romp*. Climb up blocky features to approach a short, right-facing dihedral formed by a large block. A powerful and difficult mantle move surmounts this block, then face climbing above leads to the anchors. FA: Louie Anderson 2008.

㊱ Romper Room 12b ★★ ❏

9 bolts to 2 open shuts, 27m/90'. Start as for *New Directions* and scramble to the top of the initial blocky section. The first bolt is a pre-existing bolt used by aid soloists. Unclip this after clipping the second bolt to prevent rope drag. Climb the clean slab up to the center of the roof. Turn the roof and continue on the upper headwall to an anchor at the top of the slab. Use a long draw on the roof bolt to limit rope drag. FA: Louie Anderson 2004.

㊲ Romp Direct 12a ★★★ ❏

Bolts, nuts and cams to 1 ½" to a 2-bolt belay, 26m/85'. A cleaner and more direct version of *Romp*. After climbing to the top of the starting block, climb a right-trending undercling flake to gain the thin crack above. Follow this until it intersects with the horizontal crack under the roof and finish as for *Romp*. Originally led on gear, this route now has some bolts due to the addition of adjacent sport climbs. FA: Unknown. FFA: Louie Anderson 1987.

㊳ F.U.B.A.R. 12b ★★ ❏

14 bolts to 2 open shuts, 27m/90'. Begin climbing just right of the starting dihedral of *Romp Direct*. Follow bolts up the blunt prow to reach an undercling crack and the right-trending seam above. Once you reach the roof, continue through it on manufactured holds and finish on the steep slab above. Shares anchors with *Romper Room*. FA: Gary Henning 2009.

㊴ All Tapped Out 13a ★★ ❏

12 bolts to a double ring anchor, 26m/85'. Start six feet right of *F.U.B.A.R.* Climb over a small roof and continue up the orange face to another roof. A powerful boulder problem up the shallow dihedral leads to a steep slab. The route continues through the roof above on manufactured holds and finishes up the slab. FA: Gary Henning 2009.

㊵ Love Nest 12d ★★★ ❏

12 bolts to a double ring anchor, 26m/85'. Begin climbing six feet right of *All Tapped Out*. This route climbs up the orange face to the deepest part of the low roof. A powerful boulder problem on manufactured holds leads out the roof. Continue up the steep slab between the roofs. Cross the higher roof and finish up the upper slab. Shares anchors with *All Tapped Out*. FA: Gary Henning 2009.

Slab City

Gary Henning on Love Nest (12d)

④ Bottoms Up 12c
★★ ❏

11 bolts to a double ring anchor, 27m/90'. This route starts a few feet to the right of *Love Nest* and follows the crack system on the right end of the low roof. Continue through the middle face to reach the upper roof. Climb through this on manufactured holds and continue up the face above. FA: Gary Henning 2009.

④ Gulp Swallow 10c
★★★ ❏

Bolts, nuts and cams to 2" to a 2-bolt belay, 22m/75'. Start as for *Bottoms Up,* but traverse right on the horizontal crack between the roofs and finish up the right-facing crack and flake. Once you reach the top of the crack system, stem up through the alcove to reach the anchors. The climbing does not necessarily follow the bolt line, but wanders a bit between some of the bolts. One of the better crack lines at the Quarry. Originally led on gear, this route now has some bolts due to the addition of adjacent sport climbs. FA: Unknown, but prior to 1970. FFA: Richard Jensen, Mark Smith 3-1982.

Slab City

Slab City Right

64 • Climber's Guide: Riverside Quarry

Slab City

- ㊸ Chaste, but Tasty 12a ★★
- ㊹ Lovely Lady 10c ★★★★
- ㊺ Synchronicity 11c ★★★
- ㊻ The View Line 12a ★★★
- ㊼ Pity Committee 11a ★★★
- ㊽ Pho King Freeloader 11a ★★
- ㊾ Ass Over Teacups 10d ★★
- ㊿ Utopia 10c ★★★
- 51 One for the Road 5.8 (r)

- 52 Octo-Mom 12c ★★
- 53 Baby Brigade 12b ★
- 54 Juggernaut 12b ★
- 55 White Heat 10b ★★
- 56 Groove Factor 5.9 ★★
- 57 Pleasure Dome 10b ★★
- 58 White Light 5.7 ★★
- 59 Scrawny, not Brawny 10a ★

㊸ Chaste, but Tasty 12a ★★ ☐

13 bolts to a double biner anchor, 29m/95'. This route starts eight feet right of *Gulp Swallow*. Climb up to and around the right side of the low roof and continue through thin and technical face moves to reach the right end of the upper roof. Climb right and then back left (above the roof) to finish up the slab above. FA: Gary Henning 2009.

㊹ Lovely Lady 10c ★★★★ ☐

9 bolts to a double ring anchor, 24m/80'. Start climbing eight feet right of *Chaste, but Tasty* off the top of a series of stacked blocks. Climb straight up the shallow depression, before moving right following a series of widely-spaced edges. A boulder problem at the end of this face leads up and left to join the crack of *Gulp Swallow*. Finish as for that route. This is one of the better 5.10's in the Quarry, and is not as steep or intimidating as some of the lines up on the main cliff. FA: Gary Henning 2009.

㊺ Synchronicity 11c ★★★ ☐

11 bolts to 2 open shuts, 30m/100'. Scramble to the top of some boulders 20 feet right of *Gulp Swallow*. Follow the bolted line up a shallow corner and the clean face above. After climbing through some broken terrain, finish on the upper slab. FA: Louie Anderson 2004.

㊻ The View Line 12a ★★★ ☐

13 bolts to a double chain anchor, 30m/100'. Start climbing at ground level about fifteen feet right of *Synchronicity*. Follow bolts up the stacked boulders and blocks to reach a ledge below the steep slab. Continue straight up the slab, passing a series of stepped flakes in the middle of the route. Finishes on the smooth slab above. FA: Gary Henning 2009.

㊼ Pity Committee 11a ★★★ ☐

9 bolts to 2 open shuts, 26m/85'. This route is found 20 feet right of *Synchronicity*. It starts off the top of a pile of boulders and climbs up to and over a series of small bulges, following flakes and cracks. FA: Louie Anderson 2004.

㊽ Pho King Freeloader 11a ★★ ❑

10 bolts to a double ring anchor, 26m/85'. Start five feet right of *Pity Committee* and follow bolts up the obvious left-facing flake. Continue straight over the roof above on manufactured holds. A long and enjoyable slab above leads to high anchors. FA: Dylan Henning 2010.

㊾ Ass Over Teacups 10d ★★ ❑

13 bolts to a double ring anchor, 30m/100'. One of the original Quarry routes. Start as for *Pho King Freeloader*, but after clipping the fourth bolt (with a long sling), traverse right to cross *Utopia* at its fifth bolt. Continue traversing right and follow the ramp on the right face. Join *OctoMom* at its seventh bolt and stay on that route until after clipping its eighth bolt. After clipping that bolt, move up and left to join *Utopia* again at its eighth bolt and finish on that route. FA: Richard Jensen, Mark Smith 2-1982.

㊿ Utopia 10c ★★★ ❑

13 bolts to a double ring anchor, 27m/90'. Start just right of *Ass Over Teacups* and lieback up the big left-facing flake until you can climb onto the right face. Continue up the vertical thin crack on the headwall. Once you reach the ledge, continue up the face above, climbing just left of the corner. FA (to ledge): Louie Anderson 2004. FA (with extension): Gary Henning 2010.

(51) One for the Road 5.8 (r) ❑

Nuts and cams from tiny to 2", **36m/120'**. Starting at the top anchors of *Utopia*, climb up and left on much easier terrain to the rim. Beware of a large amount of loose rock and debris encountered along the way to the top of the cliff. FA: Mark Smith, Tim Hall 12-1981.

(52) Octo-Mom 12c ★★ ❑

10 bolts to a double chain anchor, 30m/100'. Begin just right of *Utopia* and climb the steep arête. When the arête disappears, follow the slab up and right, eventually climbing through a high bulge. FA: Gary Henning 2010.

(53) Baby Brigade 12b ★ ❑

10 bolts to a double chain anchor, 30m/100'. This route starts just right of *Octo-Mom*. Climb the center of the block, finishing up the long slab above. FA: Anthony Vu 2010.

(54) Juggernaut 12b ★ ❑

5 bolts to a double ring anchor, 14m/45'. Scramble up jumbled terrain to gain a ledge system. Clip a high first bolt off a flat rail and climb the steep slab. Thin and technical. FA: Louie Anderson 2004.

(55) White Heat 10b ★★ ❑

5 bolts to a double ring anchor, 14m/45'. Located just right of *Juggernaut*. Climbs the blunt prow starting at a section of speckled, white rock. FA: Louie Anderson 2004.

(56) Groove Factor 5.9 ★★ ❑

8 bolts to a double ring anchor, 21m/70'. Follows the depression to the right of *White Heat*, passing many small ledges at the top. FA: Unknown.

Slab City

Julian Bautista on Weapons of Mass Destruction (13a)

57 Pleasure Dome
10b ★★ ☐

9 bolts to a chain anchor, 21m/70'. Begin just right of *Groove Factor* and climb the tall, diagonalling slab. An enjoyable route that tends to wander a bit. Don't be tempted to step off to the right halfway up. FA: Louie Anderson 2004.

58 White Light
5.7 ★★ ☐

6 bolts to a double ring anchor, 18m/60'. Start climbing uphill and about 5 feet right of *Pleasure Dome*. A short, left-facing corner past two bolts leads to a sloping ledge shared with *Pleasure Dome*. Clip the fourth bolt of that route and continue straight up (where that route moves right) to a large sloping ledge. Finish up the featured headwall above past three more bolts to shared anchors with *Groove Factor*. FA: Craig Britton, Chris Miller 2008.

59 Scrawny, not Brawny 10a ★ ☐
6 bolts to a double ring anchor, 12m/40'. Begin climbing just left of the far right arête off a platform of jumbled boulders. Climb up to and through shallow dihedral features. Finishes at anchors above the summit ledge. FA: Louie Anderson 2007.

Metro Sector

Metro Sector

- (60) Tagger 11d ★★★
- (61) Graffiti Wisdom 12c ★★★★★
- (62) Burly Boogie 13a ★★★
- (63) Burly Wisdom 13a ★★★★
- (64) Punk's Not Dead 12b ★★★
- (65) Pioneer Route 10d ★★
- (66) Simple Simon 11a ★★
- (67) Excuse Abuse 10a ★★
- (68) Amplified Life 11d ★★★
- (69) Weapons of Mass Destruction (W.M.D.) 13a ★★★★
- (70) Gumption 13c ★★★
- (71) Indecision 10d ★★
- (72) Rendezvous 11b ★★
- (73) Peepshow 11a ★★★
- (74) Metro 11a ★★★★
- (75) Voyeurism 11d ★★★

Located just uphill to the right of Slab City, this area is known for its blocky roofs and square cut features, all on very high quality stone. This popular area has several standout routes, including *Metro* (11a), *Tagger* (11d), *Graffiti Wisdom* (12c), and *Weapons of Mass Destruction* (13a).

Routes are described left to right, starting with those furthest downhill to the left.

(60) Tagger 11d ★★★ ❏

12 bolts to 2 open shuts, 30m/100'. Scramble up flakes at the far left of the face. After climbing through a bouldery bulge at the start continue up the steep face, staying right of the arête, to the top of the wall. FA: Louie Anderson 2004.

(61) Graffiti Wisdom 12c ★★★★★ ❏

11 bolts to 2 open shuts, 30m/100'. Climb the center of the face up to and over a small roof. Powerful climbing takes you along the small, central prow and past more roofs to finish up an exposed arête. FA: Louie Anderson 2004.

(62) Burly Boogie 13a ★★★ ❏

10 bolts to a double ring anchor, 21m/70'. Begin six feet right of *Graffiti Wisdom*. Climb up a blunt arête and over a small bulge. Continue up the steep, right-facing dihedral and finish on the arête above. FA: Louie Anderson 2007.

(63) Burly Wisdom 13a ★★★★ ❏

14 bolts to 2 open shuts, 30m/100'. A link up. Climb *Burly Boogie*, but after clipping the tenth bolt, move up and left and join *Graffiti Wisdom* at its eighth bolt. Finish on that route. FA: Louie Anderson 2007.

Metro Sector

64 Punk's Not Dead 12b
★★★ ❏

6 bolts to 2 open shuts, 17m/55'. A powerful climb that starts on the right side of the face at its namesake graffiti. The route climbs through several small bulges and is steeper and harder than it looks. FA: Louie Anderson 2003.

The following three routes climb the small formation right of Punk's Not Dead *and can be used to access the Sidewalk Ledge above.*

65 Pioneer Route 10d
★★ ❏

6 bolts to a double chain anchor, 17m/55'. Begin climbing 15 feet right of *Punk's Not Dead,* on a separate formation. Climb past two ledges and a high crux to finish at the Sidewalk Ledge. FA: Louie Anderson 2004.

66 Simple Simon 11a
★★ ❏

8 bolts to a double ring anchor, 15m/50'. This route starts downhill and 25 feet right of *Pioneer Route*. Climb the center of the formation. FA: Louie Anderson 2004.

Grahm Doe on Gumption (13b)

67 Excuse Abuse 10a ★★ ❏

7 bolts to a double ring anchor, 15m/50'. Starts off a ledge just up and right of *Simple Simon* (with a belay bolt on the left end of the ledge). Climb the right arête passing a big ledge at half-height. FA: Louie Anderson 2008.

Metro Sector

Sidewalk Ledge

This ledge is located above and right of *Punk's Not Dead*. It can be approached by scrambling up the gully to the left of *Metro*, or by climbing one of the three routes listed above. It's large enough for several people to lounge comfortably unroped. The following three routes begin from this ledge.

68 Amplified Life 11d ★★★ ❏

7 bolts to 2 open shuts, 21m/70'. The left route. Crosses a low roof before moving into the stemming corner. An exposed traverse at the end of the dihedral leads to easier climbing. FA: Louie Anderson 2004.

69 Weapons of Mass Destruction (W.M.D.) 13a ★★★★ ❏

7 bolts to 2 open shuts, 21m/70'. The middle route. Powerful climbing thankfully leads to good holds under the roof. Cruxy moves (turning the lip) on thin crimps are followed by enjoyable climbing on good holds. OB: Louie Anderson 2004. FA: Alan Moore 2005.

70 Gumption 13b ★★★ ❏

10 bolts to a double ring anchor, 27m/90'. The right route. Begin climbing about six feet right of *WMD*. Very powerful (and reachy) sequences low lead to a good shake under the first roof. From here pumpy climbing takes you over the next, bigger roof to a high deadpoint challenge. FA: Grahm Doe 2004.

71 Indecision 10d ★★ ❏

10 bolts to 2 open shuts, 27m/90'. Climb up a huge, detached flake (past 2 bolts) to gain a flat ledge. Follow the left bolt line up a corner system before moving back right to join *Rendezvous* at its eighth bolt. Finish on that route. FA: Louie Anderson 2007.

72 Rendezvous 11b ★★ ❏

9 bolts to 2 open shuts, 27m/90'. Start as for *Indecision*. Once you reach the big ledge, follow the right bolt line up to and through the notch at the top of the face. FA: Louie Anderson 2004.

73 Peepshow 11a ★★★ ❏

9 bolts to 2 open shuts, 27m/90'. A series of jumbled flakes and blocks lead off the left side of the patio to a large ledge. Follow the corner system leaving the right side of this ledge to the top of the wall. FA: Louie Anderson 2004.

74 Metro 11a ★★★★ ❏

10 bolts to 2 open shuts, 30m/100'. Start off the center of the patio on a right-facing flake. Climb over a couple of small bulges before traversing slightly left and then up into a dished rest. A final series of bulges lead to the anchors. FA: Louie Anderson 2003.

75 Voyeurism 11d ★★★ ❏

10 bolts to 2 open shuts, 30m/100'. Climb the face just left of the right arête. The poor rock found at the start gets much better after the second bolt. Harder and more sustained than the other routes on this section of wall. FA: Louie Anderson 2003.

Left of the Roof

72 • Climber's Guide: Riverside Quarry

Left of the Roof

- ⓻⓺ Flesh and Blood 11b ★★★★★
- ⓻⓻ Raging Raptor 12a ★★★★★
- ⓻⓼ Choss Goggles 12c ★★★★
- ⓻⓽ Double Agent 12a ★★★
- ⓼⓪ Double Shock 12a ★★★
- ⓼① Culture Shock 11c ★★★★
- ⓼② Choss Revolution 12c ★★★★
- ⓼③ Buzzkill 12c ★★★
- ⓼④ Hercules Hand Crack 5.8 ★
- ⓼⑤ Trundle Trophy 10c ★★★★★
- ⓼⑥ Diehard 12b ★★
- ⓼⑦ Diehard with a Vengeance 12c ★★
- ⓼⑧ Master Blaster 12c ★★
- ⓼⑨ New Frontiers 12a ★★★★
- ⓽⓪ Inspiration 11c ★★★
- ⓽① Inspirational Frontiers 12a ★★★★
- ⓽② Winds of Change 12a ★★★
- ⓽③ Inspired Change 12a ★★★★
- ⓽④ Demoralizer 11d ★★
- ⓽⑤ Fully Demoralized 12a ★★★
- ⓽⑥ Flexercise 10b ★★★★★
- ⓽⑦ Burning Desire 12c ★★★★
- ⓽⑧ Quarryman 12b ★★★
- ⓽⑨ Apocalypto 12b ★★★
- ⓵⓪⓪ Apocalypse Man 12b ★★★

This area is located just to the right of the Metro Sector. The standout routes here are the popular *Flexercise* (10b) and *Trundle Trophy* (10c), and the mega-long *Burning Desire* (12c) and *Choss Revolution* (12c). The former two are the easiest of the steeper offerings at the crag, and are extremely popular due to their steep, juggy bulges. Other not to miss routes include the neighboring *Flesh and Blood* (11b), *Raging Raptor* (12a) and *Choss Goggles* (12c).

Routes are described left to right.

⓻⓺ Flesh and Blood 11b ★★★★★ ☐

16 bolts to a double ring anchor, **34m/115' – lower with a 70-meter rope.** Begins at the left edge of the face, just right of the arête. Climb up to and traverse around the right side of a shallow roof, before cutting back left and following a series of blocky corners and flakes up the face. Near the top of the route, climb onto a sloping ledge before pulling a final bulge. FA: Louie Anderson 2005.

⓻⓻ Raging Raptor 12a ★★★★★ ☐

15 bolts to a double ring anchor, 30m/100'. Start climbing ten feet right of *Flesh and Blood*. Climb diagonally up and left and then up the center of the face passing a horizontal crack at the fourth bolt. Continue up the smooth center face, passing a sloping ledge high before tackling the pumpy final bulge. FA: Louie Anderson 2005.

⓻⓼ Choss Goggles 12c ★★★★ ☐

14 bolts to a double ring anchor, 30m/100'. Begins as for *Raging Raptor*, but where that route moves left, this one climbs straight up. Climbs over several shallow overlaps and past a small ledge at the fifth bolt. A big move high on the route leads to a good rest at the ledge before a final, awkward sequence through the upper roof. FA: Brent Webster 2005.

Left of the Roof • Route Profile

Climber: Clark Eising

Left of the Roof • Route Profile

Flesh and Blood
ROUTE PROFILE

76 Flesh and Blood 11b ★★★★★

For complete route description see page 73

As with most of the other standout routes in the Quarry, *Flesh and Blood's* popularity revolves around its multiple cruxes and the diversity of the movement found in those cruxes. It offers a little bit of everything on enjoyable, blocky rock of a very high quality. This route also has a high aesthetic value, climbing just right of a very striking arête line that is visible from quite a distance.

A traverse low approaches the powerful moves getting onto the main face. This leads to big, blocky corners and features and a long section of fun, vertical climbing. A tricky sequence onto the high slab is followed by a welcome rest that makes the final bulge a bit easier to tackle than it otherwise would be. All in all, this is a very enjoyable climb and one of the most sought after 5.11's at the crag.

Remember that lowering off of this route requires every inch of a 60-meter rope. In fact, some rope lengths require the climber to lower to the top of the boulder behind the route's start instead of the ground. If there is any doubt as to whether or not your rope will reach the ground, please use a longer rope.

Left of the Roof • Route Profile

Raging Raptor
ROUTE PROFILE

Climber: Mike Zitt

Left of the Roof • Route Profile

⓻ Raging Raptor 12a ★★★★★

For complete route description see page 73

Towards the left end of the cliff line is a beautiful section of blocky rock, with a high roof. There are three great routes on this panel of rock, but of the three, *Raging Raptor* is the best. This popular route climbs immaculate stone up the center of the tall face. Crimpy moves on the first third of the climb get climbers good and pumped before encountering the crux a little more than halfway up the route. Following the crux, a tricky maneuver onto the sloping ledge near the top of the route is rewarded with a good rest before the final roof challenge. Turning this roof is surprisingly easier than you might imagine, due to the positive holds at and just above the lip.

The route's name is more than just an exercise in alliteration. When attempting the first redpoint of the climb, the first ascentionist had a hawk repeatedly shriek and dive towards him. Above his bolt, and with nowhere to go, he was more or less trapped. Each successive dive brought the hawk closer and closer, until on the final dive the hawk struck the climber's shoulder with outstretched talons and knocked him off the route. This is the only time that something like this has happened at the crag, and while there were many theories as to why it happened, no verifiable motive was ever identified. You often hear that every scar tells a story, but some are better than others…

Left of the Roof

⑦⑨ Double Agent 12a ★★★ ❏

13 bolts to a double ring anchor, 30m/100'. This route starts fifteen feet downhill from *Choss Goggles*, at a section of gray and brown rock. Climb over a shallow flaky roof and past a crimp crux at the second bolt. Continue up the face above through several shallow bulges and ledges. FA: Louie Anderson 2007

⑧⓪ Double Shock 12a ★★★ ❏

19 bolts to a double ring anchor, **36m/120' L-P-L or lower with a 70-meter rope.** Climb *Double Agent* and after clipping the anchors of that route, traverse right to join *Culture Shock* at its thirteenth bolt. Finish up that route. FA: Louie Anderson 2007.

⑧① Culture Shock 11c ★★★★ ❏

17 bolts to a double ring anchor, **36m/120' L-P-L or lower with a 70-meter rope.** This route starts six feet to the right of *Double Agent*. Climb up right-facing flake systems before traversing up and back left onto a shallow ledge system. Climb the center of the tall face on primarily positive holds, over a series of small bulges. FA: Louie Anderson 2007.

⑧② Choss Revolution 12c ★★★★ ❏

16 bolts to a double ring anchor, **41m/135' L-P-L.** Begin climbing five feet right of *Culture Shock* at the base of a gold streaked face. Blocky holds lead over a series of bulges and past multiple cruxes. A long and popular route. Don't be tempted to stop at the 100-foot anchors, as some of the best climbing is found on the steeper headwall above them. This route can be used to approach the summit ledge at the base of *Hercules Hand Crack*. FA: Louie Anderson 2004.

⑧③ Buzzkill 12c ★★★ ❏

18 bolts to a double ring anchor, **41m/135' L-P-L.** The right route. Start climbing ten feet right of *Choss Revolution* at a right-facing flake. After clipping the eighth bolt, move up and left to join *Choss Revolution* at its seventh bolt. FA: Louie Anderson 2004.

⑧④ Hercules Hand Crack 5.8 ★ ❏

Cams from 2" to 4", 9m/30'. If this were longer, it would probably be fairly popular. As it is, it may not really be worth the effort to get to. Approach is made by walking down to the broad ledge below the crack from the summit. It can also be approached by climbing either New Frontiers or *Choss Revolution*. FA: Mark Smith, Richard Jensen 2-1982.

⑧⑤ Trundle Trophy 10c ★★★★★ ❏

13 bolts to a double ring anchor, 29m/95'. This route starts up big blocky flakes twelve feet right of *Buzzkill*. One of the easiest steep offerings at the crag, this popular route offers several rests and juggy bulges. FA: Louie Anderson 2004.

⑧⑥ Diehard 12b ★★❏

7 bolts to double ring anchor, 15m/50'. A crimpy route that climbs the center of the face, trending slightly right for the majority of the route. FA: Louie Anderson 2003.

Left of the Roof

⓼⓻ Diehard with a Vengeance 12c ★★ ❑

7 bolts to a double ring anchor, 15m/50'. Climb *Diehard* to its third bolt. From here, climb straight up on thin crimps, side pulls and underclings to reach easier terrain. FA: Willard Gove 2011.

⓼⓼ Master Blaster 12c ★★ ❑

8 bolts to double ring anchor, 15m/50'. Starting six feet right of *Diehard*, follow a series of right-facing flakes before traversing back left and joining *Diehard* at its fourth bolt. FA: Louie Anderson 2003.

⓼⓽ New Frontiers 12a ★★★★ ❑

10 bolts to 2 open shuts, 30m/100'. Located above *Diehard* and *Master Blaster*. From the anchor of those routes, climb up and left through a bulge and follow a left-facing flake to the base of a small roof. After the roof, blocky holds lead to the anchors. This route can be used to access the summit ledge at the base of *Hercules Hand Crack*. FA: Louie Anderson 2003.

⓽⓪ Inspiration 11c ★★★ ❑

8 bolts to a double ring anchor, 15m/50'. This route follows the right-facing lieback flakes found six feet right of *Master Blaster*. After clipping the fifth bolt, a crux traverse up and left leads to a prominent, triangular horn. Easier climbing leads from here to the shared anchors with *Master Blaster*. FA: Louie Anderson 2006.

⓽⓵ Inspirational Frontiers 12a ★★★★ ❑

20 bolts to a double ring anchor, **42m/140' Rappel to or L-P-L using anchors of** *Trundle Trophy*. After climbing *Inspiration*, do not clip the anchors of that route, but instead continue up and left following the bolt line of New Frontiers. FA: Louie Anderson 2007.

⓽⓶ Winds of Change 12a ★★★ ❑

14 bolts to a double ring anchor, 30m/100'. This new upper pitch is found directly above the anchors of *Inspiration*. Climb through several powerful bulges, finishing at the top of the cliff. FA: Louie Anderson 2007.

⓽⓷ Inspired Change 12a ★★★★ ❑

23 bolts to a double ring anchor, **44m/145' Rappel to or L-P-L using anchors of** *Demoralizer*. After climbing *Inspiration*, continue straight into *Winds of Change* for a very popular stamina challenge. FA: Louie Anderson 2007.

⓽⓸ Demoralizer 11d ★★ ❑

13 bolts to a double ring anchor, 30m/100'. Begin climbing six feet right of *Inspiration*. A low boulder problem leads to continuous crimpy face climbing. Finishes with steep, juggy face climbing above and right of the anchors of *Inspiration*. FA: Louie Anderson 2006.

⓽⓹ Fully Demoralized 12a ★★★ ❑

23 bolts to a double ring anchor, **44m/145' L-P-L.** After climbing *Demoralizer* and clipping its anchors, continue up and left following the bulge flakes of *Winds of Change*. FA: Louie Anderson 2007.

Trundle Trophy
Left of the Roof • Route Profile
ROUTE PROFILE

Climber: Alice Rietveld

Left of the Roof • Route Profile

Some of the blocks were stubborn, and not all of the rock was removed on that first pass. Anderson had to return with a bigger crowbar, and a car jack, to tackle the largest of the challenges. For those of you who have never had the opportunity to trundle something the size of what we're talking about here, the experience is hard to fully describe. There is a nervous anticipation of the trundle itself, but this is tempered by the need to keep yourself (and your rope) out of harm's way. Now multiply that experience by about twenty repetitions and you may start to imagine the adrenaline coursing through Anderson's body on those couple of days.

Perhaps no route at the cliff had more loose rock removed from it than this one, but at the end of all of that trundling, he got his trophy...

85 Trundle Trophy 10c ★★★★★

For complete route description see page 78

Easily the most climbed route in the Quarry. The proliferation of good rests (often no-hands) found over the length of the climb, allow climbers to tackle the many steep bulges that might not be able to otherwise. Of course, all of those rests are also the main reason for the recent grade change. While some will be bummed to have lost their first 10d, this route is much better positioned as a 10c.

Prior to its first ascent, this particular section of cliff was covered in huge, loose blocks and flakes. The steepness of the line was appealing, but no one wanted to tackle all of that loose rock. Finally, Louie Anderson decided that the time had come. He rappelled in from the top of the cliff and proceeded to tackle the veritable time bomb of loose stone.

Left of the Roof

⁹⁶ Flexercise 10b ★★★★★ ❏

11 bolts to a double ring anchor, 29m/95'. Begin climbing at the fault line just right of *Demoralizer*. A fun and popular route, offering sustained, moderate climbing with a steep and airy stemming finish. FA: Louie Anderson 2006.

⁹⁷ Burning Desire 12c ★★★★ ❏

23 bolts to a double ring anchor, **48m/160'**. This route starts ten feet downhill from *Flexercise*. Crimpy and powerful moves lead up the lower face, over a series of small overlaps to a recessed ledge system in the middle of the route. From here, steep bulges lead to the final headwall, where you are forced to do big moves leading up and right to the summit anchors. Shares the last few bolts with *Quarryman*. **Caution: Rappel to the 100-foot anchors or L-P-L using a 70-meter rope.** FA: Louie Anderson 2006.

⁹⁸ Quarryman 12b ★★★ ❏

22 bolts to a double ring anchor, **50m/165'**. This popular route acts as the initiation for all aspiring Quarry Masters. It starts ten feet right of Burning Desire and climbs through a series of small bulges before dealing with the first of many cruxes. Follow the bolts as they weave their way to the top of the cliff. At 165 feet long, this is one of the longest single pitches at the Quarry, and although there are several cruxes, there are enough good rests to keep the pump at bay. **Caution: Rappel to the 100-foot anchors or L-P-L using a 70-meter rope.** FA: Louie Anderson 2003.

⁹⁹ Apocalypto 12b ★★★ ❏

9 bolts to a double ring anchor, 24m/80'. Begin as for *Quarryman*, but after clipping the second bolt move up and right, following the blunt prow system. A powerful deadpoint after the fourth bolt is the crux on this short route, which is more difficult than it appears. FA: Louie Anderson 2007.

¹⁰⁰ Apocalypse Man 12b ★★★ ❏

23 bolts to a double ring anchor, **50m/165'**. After climbing *Apocalypto* and clipping its anchors, move up and left to join *Quarryman* at its tenth bolt. Finish on that route. **Caution: Rappel to the 100-foot anchors or L-P-L using a 70-meter rope.** FA: Louie Anderson 2007.

Audrey Harris on Inspiration (11c)

Roof Area

Roof Area

- ⑩ Nostalgia 11c ★★★★★
- ⑩ Swank Nostalgia 12a ★★★★★
- ⑩ The Ultimate 12d ★★★★★
- ⑩ False Alarm 12d ★★★★
- ⑩ Hanging by a Thread 12b ★★★★★
- ⑩ Swan Song 11b ★★★
- ⑩ Swan Hang 12b ★★★★
- ⑩ Pursuit of Pain 11d ★★★★
- ⑩ Triple Trouble 12c ★★★
- ⑩ Leviathan 11d ★★★★★
- ⑪ Big Bang 12d ★★★
- ⑫ The Zone 12b ★★★★★
- ⑬ Critical Mass 12c ★★★★
- ⑭ Vendetta 12b ★★★
- ⑮ Angst 11c ★★
- ⑯ Cave Troll 12d (r) ★★★
- ⑰ Exposure 12b (r) ★★★★
- ⑱ Gollum 12c ★★★
- ⑲ Balrog 12b ★★★
- ⑳ Delirious 11b ★★★★
- ㉑ Epiphany 11c ★★
- ㉒ Salutations 11b ★★★
- ㉓ Déjà vu 11d ★★★
- ㉔ Catch 22 12a ★★★
- ㉕ American Dream 11b ★★★, 10a ★★, 11b ★★★★, 11c ★★★
- ㉖ Mojo 13b ★★★
- ㉗ Trepanation 12c ★★★★

Roof Area • Route Profile

Climber: Nikki Chau

Nostalgia
ROUTE PROFILE

101 Nostalgia 11c ★★★★★

For complete route description see page 86.

All of the routes found on this narrow, golden face are excellent. *Nostalgia* being the easiest of the three primary routes means that it sees the most traffic, if for no other reason than it being more accessible to a broader range of climbers. It's hard to argue with the quality of the climbing however, and that is certainly another reason for its popularity.

The entry moves are challenging enough to grab one's attention right from the beginning, and other than a short section in the middle of the route, the climbing remains engaging right to the anchors. Each of the more difficult sections encountered on the route is far different than the next, and that diversity is one of this route's best traits. The fact that the rock quality is immaculate for the majority of the route is equally appealing.

A fine blend of power, endurance and technical ability are required to succeed on this very popular climb. If you're up for the challenge, make sure to save a little for the pumpy moves right before the anchor.

Roof Area

The area is found just right of the Left of the Roof area. One of the most popular areas at the crag, The Roof Area offers slightly steeper climbing, with some wildly exposed roof routes above. There are many popular routes to be found here, with the standouts being *Nostalgia* (11c), *Leviathan* (11d), *Hanging by a Thread* (12b), *The Zone* (12c), *Exposure* (12b) and *The Ultimate* (12d). It is also home to the classic multi-pitch route, *American Dream* (11b, 10a, 11b, 11c).

Routes are described left to right.

101 Nostalgia 11c ★★★★★ ☐

11 bolts to 2 open shuts, 30m/100'. This route is found at the far left of the golden face. Climb up to a right-facing flake and continue up to and over a small roof. Follow a left-facing flake system to the final bulge. This is the popular approach pitch for *Pursuit of Pain*. FA: Louie Anderson 2005.

102 Swank Nostalgia 12a ★★★★★ ☐

21 bolts to a double ring anchor, **46m/155' L-P-L.** After climbing *Nostalgia* and clipping its anchor, climb up and right (passing over a few small bulges) to gain a left-facing corner system high on the wall. One of the best long routes at the crag, with good climbing right till the anchors. FA: Louie Anderson 2005.

103 The Ultimate 12d ★★★★★ ☐

12 bolts to a double ring anchor, 30m/100'. This route starts eight feet right of *Nostalgia* and follows the featured ramp up and right. Climb through a difficult boulder problem, passing the third bolt. Continue up the center of the face on fairly sustained climbing. FA: Louie Anderson 2011.

104 False Alarm 12d ★★★★ ☐

12 bolts to 2 open shuts, 30m/100'. A link-up. Begin as for *The Ultimate*, but after clipping that route's fourth bolt move up and right to join *Hanging by a Thread* at its fifth bolt. FA: Louie Anderson 2003.

105 Hanging by a Thread 12b ★★★★★ ☐

14 bolts to 2 open shuts, 30m/100'. Begin climbing twelve feet right of *The Ultimate* and climb through several small bulges. Decent rests in the middle of the route give you a little back in time for a committing sequence just before the anchors. One of the best at the crag. FA: Louie Anderson 2003.

106 Swan Song 11b ★★★ ☐

10 bolts to a double ring anchor, 21m/70'. This route starts eight feet right of *Hanging by a Thread*. Climb straight up the fault line to a flake roof. After passing this roof, move up and left and follow the right-facing flake system. A high crux guards the anchors. FA: Louie Anderson 2011.

107 Swan Hang 12b ★★★★ ☐

15 bolts to two open shuts, 30m/100'. A link-up. Climb *Swan Song*, but after clipping the anchors of that right, climb up and left to join *Hanging by a Thread* at its eleventh bolt and finish on that route. FA: Louie Anderson 2011.

Roof Area

(108) Pursuit of Pain 11d ★★★★ ☐

11 bolts to a double ring anchor, 26m/85'. Named for the original aid test piece that once finished up the same general line of climbing, this route is found above *Hanging by a Thread*. Approach the climb by climbing *Nostalgia*. From the anchors of that route, traverse right and up onto the slab. Belay from the right bolted anchor so as to be out of the way of the leader. Climb the right side of the hanging block and the clean, steep face above it. Finishes out the right side of the high roof. **Use caution when lowering from the slab belay with a 60-meter rope.** FA: Louie Anderson 2008.

(109) Triple Trouble 12c ★★★ ☐

14 bolts to a double chain anchor, 30m/100'. Starts at the shallow left-facing dihedral 15 feet right of *Hanging by a Thread*. After clipping the second bolt move left and climb up to and over a low roof. Continue up the left side of the face, passing two more bulges. FA: Louie Anderson 2005.

(110) Leviathan 11d ★★★★★ ☐

13 bolts to 2 open shuts, 30m/100'. Begin as for *Triple Trouble*, but after clipping the second bolt continue up the center of the face. Follow discontinuous, left-facing flakes all the way to the top of the wall. Pumpy and popular. Use a long draw on, or skip, the third bolt to limit rope drag. This is the popular approach pitch for *Big Bang* and *The Zone*. FA: Louie Anderson 2004.

(111) Big Bang 12d ★★★ ☐

10 bolts to a double ring anchor, 27m/90'. Approached by climbing Leviathan. Climb up and left from the slab belay. Underclings in the roof lead to a big throw to the edge around the lip. Engaging moves on big holds continue up the headwall. Use a long sling on the roof bolt to limit rope drag. **BEWARE – extreme rope stretcher to get to the ground from the slab anchors with a doubled 60-meter rope!** FA: Louie Anderson 2004.

(112) The Zone 12b ★★★★★ ☐

12 bolts to a double ring anchor, 27m/90'. Approached by climbing *Leviathan*. Climb up and right from the slab belay. Flakes lead out the roof to a committing lip sequence. Positive edges take you up the slightly overhung headwall. A very good route that provides the most popular passage through the roof. Use a long sling on the roof bolt to limit rope drag. The second roof bolt is intended as a dogging/work bolt only. **BEWARE – extreme rope stretcher to get to the ground from the slab anchors with a doubled 60-meter rope!** FA: Louie Anderson 2004.

(113) Critical Mass 12c ★★★★ ☐

13 bolts to 2 open shuts, 30m/100'. This route starts ten feet right of *Leviathan*. Start climbing off the top of the big, flat rock lying on the ground. Climb past a series of crisp edges and rails to a hard boulder problem at the overlap. Finish up left-facing flakes on easier, but exciting terrain. Shares the last bolt and anchors with Leviathan. . FA: Louie Anderson 2004.

(114) Vendetta 12b ★★★ ☐

13 bolts to a double ring anchor, 29m/95'. This route begins eight feet right of *Critical Mass*, next to the large boulder. Climb onto a low ledge and continue up right-facing flakes. A crux sequence over a bulge at forty feet leads to easier climbing on positive features. FA: Louie Anderson 2006.

Roof Area • Route Profile

Hanging by a Thread
ROUTE PROFILE

Climber: Valarie Heredia

Roof Area • Route Profile

105 Hanging by a Thread 12b ★★★★★

For complete route description see page 86

Perhaps the most sought after difficult route in the Quarry, and with good reason. This line would be a standout route at just about any crag you chose to visit. Multiple difficult sections are found on this route, with a distinct low crux and another at the top of the route. The balance of the climbing, while easier, still has its challenges. Thankfully, a good rest exists on the sloping ledge two-thirds of the way up the route.

Originally more mentally challenging, this route is now a little safer due to the fact that the first ascentionist returned and reworked the bolt spacing. What originally was an eleven-bolt route, now sports fourteen bolts. That's not to say though that there aren't still some exciting sections. It is definitely at the high end of the grade.

The name of this route (as do many) has a good story behind it. While rappelling in from the top of the cliff to perform the initial cleaning and bolting efforts, a lot of swinging back and forth was required to access the different portions of the route. Once the work was completed for that first day, the climber was jumaring back to the top of the cliff when he saw an obviously damaged section of rope, where it had abraded against a sharp edge of rock. What to do? Would it be better to rappel off slowly or to continue jumaring gingerly up the rope to gain the summit where the rope was anchored? The decision was made to continue upward. Once the damaged section was reached, it was discovered that the rope was damaged far worse than first thought. In fact less than half of the rope's inner core strands were still intact. The climber was quite literally "hanging by a thread." Once this section was passed, all was safe again and shortly thereafter this Quarry classic saw its first redpoint.

Climber's Guide: Riverside Quarry

The Zone
ROUTE PROFILE

Climber: Matt Hulet

112 The Zone 12b ★★★★★

For complete route description see page 87

Many of the climbers who frequent the Quarry never climb any of the extension pitches. While there are a multitude of quality routes that start and end on the ground, and don't require hanging belays, limiting one's self to those routes prevents a climber from truly appreciating all that the crag has to offer. There are many extensions and second pitch options in the Quarry, but *The Zone* has to be one of the most popular.

A short bit of slab climbing leads to the roof. There are some close together bolts in the roof itself, but it's best to skip the first one and use a longer draw on the second. You may not feel secure enough to do this on your onsight attempt, but most people redpoint the route this way once they know the moves. If you clip both bolts, you'll pay the price with a little extra rope drag by the time you're nearing the end of the climb.

The crux of the climb comes via the powerful sequence to gain the hold at the lip of the roof. However, while challenging, this move is just the beginning of the crux. The true difficulty revolves around the next few moves. Once established around the lip, a long and edge-filled headwall provides quality climbing at a more reasonable 5.11 level.

If the grade is attainable, this one should not be missed!

Roof Area

The following routes are found to the right of a large boulder that doesn't quite touch the base of the main wall.

🅕 Angst 11c ★★ ❏

11 bolts to a double ring anchor, 30m/100'. Begin as for *Gollum*, but after clipping the fourth bolt follow a diagonal rail up and left. Climb through the bulge and continue on big edges to the anchors. This is the approach route for those intending to climb *Cave Troll* or *Exposure* above. FA: Louie Anderson 2004.

🅖 Cave Troll 12d (r) ★★★ ❏

12 bolts to a double chain anchor, 30m/100'. This route is approached by climbing *Angst*. Begin up the delicate slab to a funky lip encounter. Climb through the big roof and continue up the steep headwall on primarily positive holds. A very exposed and heady adventure. FA: Grahm Doe 2003.

🅗 Exposure 12b (r) ★★★★ ❏

15 bolts to a double ring anchor, 30m/100'. This route is approached by climbing *Angst*. From the hanging belay, climb up and right, following a series of fractures in the slab. Clip the bolt at the lip of the roof and jump right to the large block. A powerful and exposed boulder problem leads up and right through the roof and ultimately to better holds. Fun climbing, on mainly positive holds, leads up the long headwall to anchors at the top of the cliff. Lower from the top anchors to a hanging belay at the anchors of *Balrog*. Once your partner cleans the diagonalling line, lower him to those same anchors and rappel to the ground. FA: Louie Anderson 2011.

🅘 Gollum 12c ★★★ ❏

10 bolts to a double ring anchor, 29m/95'. Start climbing at a smooth, sloping shelf and follow right-facing features up the middle of the face. The anchors are guarded by a devious undercling crux. FA: Grahm Doe 2003.

🅙 Balrog 12b ★★★ ❏

9 bolts to a triple ring anchor, 27m/90'. A great route that starts just right of *Gollum*. Climb the clean, slightly overhung face to a high, powerful crux. FA: Grahm Doe 2003.

🅚 Delirious 11b ★★★★ ❏

11 bolts to a double ring anchor, 26m/85'. This route starts eight feet right of *Balrog*, just left of a chossy arête. Climb up onto the sloping ramp and continue up the steep face on positive flakes. Interesting moves in a corner system lead to the crux bulge and the juggy finish. Very popular. FA: Louie Anderson 2006.

Steve Edwards on *Balrog* (12b)

Roof Area

⑫ Epiphany 11c ★★ ❏

11 bolts to 2 open shuts, 30m/100'. Begin five feet right of the arête and climbs the face just to its right. After clipping the 8th bolt move right to join and finish on *Salutations*. FA: Louie Anderson 2004.

⑫ Salutations 11b ★★★ ❏

10 bolts to 2 open shuts, 29m/95'. Climb onto the low ledge and continue up the center of the face. A juggy bulge in the middle of the route makes this a popular route. FA: Louie Anderson 2004.

⑫ Déjà vu 11d ★★★ ❏

10 bolts to 2 open shuts, 30m/100'. A link-up. Start as for *Catch 22,* but after clipping that route's 5th bolt climb up and left, passing one independent bolt, before joining *Salutations* at its 7th bolt. FA: Louie Anderson 2004.

⑫ Catch 22 12a ★★★ ❏

8 bolts to 2 open shuts, 27m/90'. This route begins where the base starts to slope uphill, and follows a series of right-facing flakes to a clean, steep face. A powerful bulge high leads to a delicate finish. FA: Louie Anderson 2004.

⑫ American Dream 11b ★★★ ❏, 10a ★★ ❏, 11b ★★★★ ❏, 11c ★★★ ❏

Pitch One: 8 bolts to a double ring anchor, 27m/90'. Climb the ramp six feet right of *Catch 22* passing a positive flake. After clipping the third bolt climb straight up the steep wall left of the corner. Pitch Two: 7 bolts to a double ring anchor, 15m/50'. Move right from the belay. After clipping the slab bolt follow the clean dihedral. At the top of the dihedral, climb up and over its right side to the anchor. Pitch Three: 8 bolts to a triple ring anchor, 18m/60'. Climb up and right from the belay and follow the traversing crack under the roof. Pitch Four: 6 bolts to 2 open shuts, 20m/65'. From the belay climb up and left on the ever-steepening and increasingly difficult headwall. Lower back to the belay from the shuts. For the true multi-pitch and summit experience climb past the shuts and clip two additional bolts on your way to ring anchors on the ledge above. **If going all the way to the true summit, exercise caution as the last few feet are usually covered in loose dirt.** Descent: Either walk off or rappel (85') to the third pitch anchors. From here another rappel (100') puts you back on the ground. FA: Louie Anderson 2004.

⑫ Mojo 13b ★★★ ❏

21 bolts to 2 open shuts, **45m/150' L-P-L.** A very diverse route that tests how well rounded of a climber you are. Starts off the top of the big boulder. Balancy climbing leads to a very delicate moves on the polished slab. If you make it past the slab, you'll be challenged by difficult moves to the lip of the first bulge, followed by continuous 5.11 climbing. A final boulder problem (at 140 feet) tests your stamina just before the shuts. FA: Louie Anderson 2004.

⑫ Trepanation 12c ★★★★ ❏

20 bolts to a double ring anchor, **45m/150' L-P-L.** Climb the arête to the right of **Mojo** all the way to the top of the cliff, finishing up the drill flute. There are some sections of poor quality rock, but the climbing is fun nevertheless. Lower to the 100-foot anchors on *Mojo* to get down. FA: Brent Webster 2004.

Alex Thayer clipping on pitch two (10a)

Roof Area • Route Profile

125 American Dream

Four pitches rated:
11b ★★★
10a ★★
11b ★★★★
11c ★★★

For complete route description see page 93

The diversity of the climbing found on each pitch, and the fact that *American Dream* offers the Quarry climber a true multi-pitch experience, makes this route worthy of profiling. If you feel like trying something other than the standard one-pitch sport route, give the route a go – you won't be disappointed.

The route's second and third pitches were first led on gear, and a handful of climbers repeated the route in that form. Early in 2011, the first ascensionist returned and retro-bolted those pitches to make them more accessible to a broader group of climbers. In the first few months after the retro-bolting, the route saw far more ascents than in all the prior years combined.

Although, you can actually top out and walk off the summit, it's safer to rappel or lower from the top anchors and continue to rappel the route. The exposed dirt slope found between the upper anchors and the true summit is usually loose and dirty and can be a bit scary to cross. If you choose to top out, **please be careful.**

Alex Thayer on pitch four (11c)

American Dream
ROUTE PROFILE

Roof Area • Route Profile

Valarie Heredia on pitch three (11b)

Roof Area • Route Profile

Valarie Heredia on pitch one (11b)

Right of the Roof

98 • Climber's Guide: Riverside Quarry

Right of the Roof

- ⑫⑧ Atlas 11b ★★★
- ⑫⑨ Weight of the World 13c ★★★★★
- ⑬⓪ Salubrious 11c ★★★★
- ⑬① A Sobriquet for Salubrious Slander 12c ★★★
- ⑬② Miscreant 13b ★★★
- ⑬③ La Bella Donna 12d ★★★★★
- ⑬④ Survival of the Fittest 12a ★★★★
- ⑬⑤ Natural Selection 12c ★★★★★
- ⑬⑥ Consuming Selection 12c ★★★★
- ⑬⑦ Consumption 13c ★★★★
- ⑬⑧ Grooverider 2010 11d ★★★
- ⑬⑨ Redrum 2010 12c ★★★
- ⑭⓪ The Shining 12c ★★★★
- ⑭① Stranger than Friction 12b ★★★★
- ⑭② Sweet Surrender 12b ★★★
- ⑭③ Sweet Static 12b ★★★★
- ⑭④ Ground Zero 11a ★★★
- ⑭⑤ Automatic Static 11b ★★★★

This area is found just to the right of the Roof Area. One of the most popular sections of the cliff, this area offers quality climbing and some of the shortest steep routes at the crag. The better routes in this area include *Automatic Static* (11b), *Salubrious* (11c), *Survival of the Fittest* (12a), *Natural Selection* (12c), *Consumption* (13c), and *Weight of the World* (13c).

James Saito on Weight of the World (13c)

Right of the Roof

Don Welsh on Redrum 2010 (12c)

The routes are described left to right.

ⓘ Atlas 11b ★★★ ❏

7 bolts to a double ring anchor, 23m/75'. Begin climbing eight feet right of *Trepanation's* arête. Climb up the ramped slab until you can get on top of the obvious blocky to the left. Clip the high bolt and climb up and right around the roof. After clipping the second bolt, move up and left and climb the scooped face on primarily positive holds. FA: Louie Anderson 2006.

ⓘ Weight of the World 13c ★★★★★ ❏

19 bolts to a double ring anchor, **42m/140' L-P-L.** Climb *Atlas* and after clipping that route's anchors, continue up the center of the face past a reachy boulder problem. Another boulder problem immediately following the first guards the 100' anchors. Continue up the steep headwall above to the high anchors. FA: Louie Anderson 2006.

ⓘ Salubrious 11c ★★★★ ❏

11 bolts to a double chain anchor, 29m/95'. This route starts the same as for *Atlas*, but after clipping the second bolt, continue up and right, more or less following the line of the faint seam and dihedral. After clipping the eighth bolt, move right to the obvious horn and deadpoint to a hidden hold above. Finish up the obvious right-facing lieback flake. FA: Gary Henning 2005.

Right of the Roof

⓭ A Sobriquet for Salubrious Slander 12c ★★★ ☐
18 bolts to a double chain anchor, **44m,145' L-P-L.** Climb *Salubrious* and after clipping that route's anchors, continue up and left through bulges up the steep headwall. FA: Gary Henning 2005.

⓭ Miscreant 13b ★★★ ☐
13 bolts a double chain anchor, 29m/95'. Begin climbing six feet right of *Salubrious* and climb up the center of the face. A series of boulder problems lead to a roof at mid-height. Thin crimping above this roof leads to the eleventh bolt. After clipping this, move up and left to join *Salubrious* for its last two bolts. It is also possible to extend this route by climbing the upper portion of *A Sobriquet for Salubrious Slander*. FA: Gary Henning 2005.

⓭ La Bella Donna 12d ★★★★★ ☐
18 bolts to a double biner anchor, 45m/150 L-P-L. This route starts eight feet right of *Miscreant*. Climb the right edge of the face on very clean stone, up to and over a roof. Continue up the crimpy headwall before moving right and following the upper runnel. A very technical and popular route. FA: Gary Henning 2005.

⓭ Survival of the Fittest 12a ★★★★ ☐
13 bolts to a double ring anchor, 27m/90'. Fifteen feet right of *La Bella Donna* is a streaked face. This route climbs that face. Once established on the face, move up and left on sustained climbing to a unique crux at the upper bulge. An extremely fun route that is more about pump management than dealing with singular hard moves. FA: Louie Anderson 2006.

⓭ Natural Selection 12c ★★★★★ ☐
14 bolts to a double ring anchor, 30m/100'. This route starts the same as *Survival of the Fittest*, but climbs right from the start. A technical and difficult sequence low leads to easier climbing through the middle of the route. However, make sure to save some strength for the higher crux and pumpy moves right before the anchors. A very popular route. FA: Louie Anderson 2004.

⓭ Consuming Selection 12c ★★★★ ☐
15 bolts to a double ring anchor, 30m/100'. A link up. Climb *Consumption* to its thirteenth bolt, before moving up and left (passing one independent bolt) to join *Natural Selection* at its thirteenth bolt. Finish on that route. FA: Louie Anderson 2011.

⓭ Consumption 13c ★★★★ ☐
15 bolts to a double ring anchor, 30m/100'. Begin eight feet right of *Natural Selection*. This fun route climbs past stepped flakes before crossing a small roof. Sustained climbing leads up the wall and a traverse right to the top arête claims many would be sends just before the anchors. FA: Louie Anderson 2004.

⓭ Grooverider 2010 11d ★★★ ☐
8 bolts to a double ring anchor, 18m/60'. Begin uphill from the start of *Consumption* on top of the talus platform. Climb up the slender pillar and after clipping the third bolt, move right onto the face. Balancey and technical climbing leads to a big move. FA: Louie Anderson 2010.

Right of the Roof

In the Spring of 2010, quite a lot of loose rock was removed from the section of cliff that is home to the following routes. This was done with the intent of removing potentially dangerous flakes and to make this section of cliff safer and more solid. As the initial flakes were removed, it was realized that many surrounding panels of rock were interlocked and needed to come off as well to truly make things safe and secure. When the dust settled, five routes had more or less had their bottom 30-40 feet "exfoliated." The newly exposed layer of rock in this area was then bolted and new routes established. The five ground level routes from *Grooverider* to *Ground Zero* (in the old guidebook) are no more. In their place, there are now the routes *Grooverider 2010*, *Redrum 2010*, *Stranger Than Friction*, *Sweet Surrender*, and a slightly altered *Ground Zero*. All of these newer routes are better and more solid than their predecessors – please enjoy them.

(139) Redrum 2010 12c ★★★ ❏

7 bolts to a double ring anchor, 17m/55'. Start climbing ten feet right of *Grooverider 2010*. Three bolts of easier climbing leads to a series of crimpy and sequential moves. A powerful route that seems to be pretty popular. This route can be extended by climbing *The Shining* above. FA: Louie Anderson 2010.

(140) The Shining 12c ★★★★ ❏

15 bolts to a double ring anchor, 30m/100'. This route is traditionally climbed as an extension to *Redrum 2010*, but can also be approached by climbing *Grooverider 2010*. After clipping the anchors of your approach pitch, continue up and right following a series of flakes as they then climb up and left, turning into an undercling traverse. At the end of this traverse an improbable move right provides the crux of this extension and the failure point for those that don't have the sequence properly figured out. FA: Louie Anderson 2007.

(141) Stranger than Friction 12b ★★★★ ❏

13 bolts to a double ring anchor, 30m/100'. Starts off the top of the large, ground level flake and climbs straight up the center of the wall. Finish up the obvious right-facing dihedral. FA: Louie Anderson 2010.

(142) Sweet Surrender 12b ★★★ ❏

8 bolts to a double ring anchor, 17m/55'. Begin climbing on the right side of the big, ground-level flake. Follow a shallow corner system to the top of the subtle pillar feature. A short boulder problem leads to the overlap and easier climbing. Route finishes on the ledge halfway up the wall. FA: Louie Anderson 2010.

(143) Sweet Static 12b ★★★★ ❏

14 bolts to a double ring anchor, 30m/100'. A link up. Climb *Sweet Surrender* and then move right on the ledge to join *Automatic Static* at its tenth bolt. Finish as for that route. FA: Louie Anderson 2010.

(144) Ground Zero 11a ★★★ ❏

8 bolts to a double ring anchor, 17m/55'. Starting eight feet right of *Sweet Surrender*, climb thin flakes up to a balancey transition to a small overlap. Climb through this and finish up the high dihedral and the short slab above. The top can be done a few different ways.
FA: Louie Anderson 2005.

Right of the Roof

Andy Voss on The Shining (12c)

145 Automatic Static 11b ★★★★ ☐

16 bolts to a double ring anchor, 30m/100'. Climb *Ground Zero,* but do not clip that route's anchors. Instead traverse left on the ledge to its middle and follow the line of bolts up the center of the upper face. The route trends slightly left as it climbs. A fun route and a great way to get in a longer climb that isn't too difficult. FA: Louie Anderson 2006.

Torture Machine Area

104 • Climber's Guide: Riverside Quarry

Torture Machine Area

- (146) **Power Play 10b** ★★
- (147) **Whammy 10a** ★★
- (148) **Double Whammy 11b** ★★★
- (149) **Minimizer 10a** ★★
- (150) **Maximizer 11d** ★★★★
- (151) **Maximum Whammy 11b** ★★★
- (152) **Nemesis 12c** ★★★★
- (153) **Wonderstuff 10c** ★★★
- (154) **Bird of Prey 12c** ★★★
- (155) **Torture Machine 12b** ★★★
- (156) **House of Pain 12a** ★★★
- (157) **Adrenaline 12a** ★★
- (158) **Conundrum 11a** ★★★
- (159) **Full Conundrum 11c** ★★★
- (160) **Tangerine Dream 10d** ★★★★★
- (161) **Technicolor Tango 12c** ★★★★
- (162) **Vertigo 13a** ★★★★

This area is found directly at the top of the main climber's trail and is easily identified by locating the bright orange streak of *Tangerine Dream*. It is just right of the Right of the Roof area. This area is quite popular due to its standout routes like *Tangerine Dream* (10d), *Double Whammy* (11b), *Torture Machine* (12b), *Technicolor Tango* (12c), *Nemesis* (12c), and *Vertigo* (13a).

The routes are described left to right.

(146) Power Play 10b ★★ ❏

7 bolts to a double ring anchor, 15m/50'. This route starts five feet right of *Ground Zero* and climbs straight up the left edge of the face. Difficult moves down low lead to much easier climbing. The route can be extended into *Double Whammy*. FA: Louie Anderson 2005.

(147) Whammy 10a ★★ ❏

7 bolts to a double ring anchor, 17m/55.. Twenty feet right of *Ground Zero* is a left-leaning ramp system. Follow this to fun climbing on big edges. FA: Louie Anderson 2005.

(148) Double Whammy 11b ★★★ ❏

16 bolts to a double ring anchor, 30m/100'. The extension to *Whammy*. Climb that route and after clipping its anchors, continue straight up the wall. A crux section midway up the wall leads to a surprisingly easy passage through the top roof. Many people choose to begin on *Power Play* instead. FA: Louie Anderson 2005.

(149) Minimizer 10a ★★ ❏

7 bolts to a double ring anchor, 15m/50'. Begin as for *Whammy*, but after clipping the first bolt, climb straight up the face. After clipping the sixth bolt move left to clip the last bolt of *Whammy* and finish on that route's anchors. FA: Louie Anderson 2005.

Torture Machine Area

150 Maximizer 11d ★★★★ ☐

15 bolts to a double ring anchor, 30m/100'. Climb *Minimizer*, but after clipping the sixth bolt, continue straight up. A ledge in the middle of the route will provide a much needed rest in order to be fresh for the final crux traverse shortly before the anchors. FA: Louie Anderson 2005.

151 Maximum Whammy 11b ★★★ ☐

15 bolts to a double ring anchor, 30m/100'. A link up. Climb *Maximizer*, but after clipping the eleventh bolt climb left (passing one independent bolt) to join *Double Whammy* at its twelfth bolt. Finish on that route. FA: Louie Anderson 2005.

152 Nemesis 12c ★★★★ ☐

16 bolts to a double ring anchor, **35m/115' – lower with a 70-meter rope**. Just right of *Whammy*, follow a series of right-facing flakes up to the first of several bulges. A very good route with rests after each of the major bulges. Even with those rests though, this is at the high end of the grade. FA: Louie Anderson 2005.

153 Wonderstuff 10c ★★★ ☐

7 bolts to a double ring anchor, 15m/50'. This route starts eight feet right of *Nemesis* and climbs up right-facing flakes. After passing through steeper terrain in the middle of the route, finish up the dihedral. FA: Louie Anderson 2006.

154 Bird of Prey 12c ★★★ ☐

13 bolts to a double ring anchor, 30m/100'. Named in honor of the difficult aid route that used to more or less climb the line of *Torture Machine*. Begin climbing twenty feet right of *Wonderstuff* at the left edge of a section of white rock. Follow a line of right-facing flakes to the fourth bolt. After clipping this, move up and left to ultimately cross the high roof on its left end. FA: Louie Anderson 2006.

155 Torture Machine 12b ★★★ ☐

13 bolts to a double chain anchor, 30m/100'. Starts as for *Bird of Prey*, but after clipping the fourth bolt, move slightly right and climb up the center of the streaked face, following a very thin vertical seam to a high roof. A powerful crux at the roof leads to easier terrain and the anchors. FA: Grahm Doe 2003.

156 House of Pain 12a ★★★ ☐

13 bolts to a double ring anchor, 30m/100'. This route begins twelve feet right of *Torture Machine* and follows the right of two parallel seams. Crosses the high roof at its right end. Save some gas for the final crimp moves. FA: Louie Anderson 2005.

157 Adrenaline 12a ★★ ☐

9 bolts to a double ring anchor, 18m/60'. Start climbing fifteen feet right of *House of Pain*, just right of the pit. Follow ramp features up and left on easy terrain to reach the steep arête. Climb the steep right side of the arête. FA: Louie Anderson 2005.

158 Conundrum 11a ★★★ ☐

10 bolts to a double ring anchor, 18m/60'. Begin just right of *Adrenaline* and follow the left edge

Torture Machine Area

John Ford on Technicolor Tango (12c)

of the orange-stained white dike. After clipping the fourth bolt, move up and left climbing the recessed face up to and over a juggy bulge. FA: Louie Anderson 2005.

159 Full Conundrum 11c ★★★ ❏

13 bolts to a double ring anchor, 26m/85'. Climb *Conundrum*, but after clipping its anchors, continue straight up the corner, past two bolts, before moving right to the anchors of *Tangerine Dream*. FA: Louie Anderson 2009.

160 Tangerine Dream 10d ★★★★★ ❏

11 bolts to a double ring anchor, 26m/85'. Start as for *Conundrum*, but after clipping the fourth bolt, move up and right following the orange streak. Follow steep flakes through a bulge at the top. One of the most popular routes at the crag. FA: Louie Anderson 2005.

161 Technicolor Tango 12c ★★★★ ❏

13 bolts to two open shuts, 30m/100'. Begin climbing just right of the orange streak. Balancy and technical climbing for the first three bolts leads to a no hands rest and easier climbing in the middle of the route. The steep, blocky climbing on the upper half of the route is the reason for this route's well-deserved popularity. FA: Louie Anderson 2004.

162 Vertigo 13a ★★★★ ❏

14 bolts to two open shuts, 30m/100'. This route starts 12 feet right of *Technicolor Tango* and climbs up a vertical corner system, before committing to the sustained (and steep) climbing above. Very good moves on extremely clean rock. Shares the finishing moves of *Technicolor Tango*. FA: Louie Anderson 2004.

Roof Area • Route Profile

160 Tangerine Dream 10d
★★★★★

For complete route description see page 107

The quality of this great route ensures it popularity, but the fact that it sits right at the top of the main climber's trail doesn't hurt either. Of course on top of those attributes, it is also the most colorful piece of rock at the crag. This makes it a very aesthetically pleasing line and one that is often photographed.

Comparably easy climbing leads to the base of the obvious orange streak. Sequential and challenging moves up the central prow often baffle climbers before a short section of easier climbing leads to a great ledge rest. From here, steep moves lead up and right off the ledge to the steep flake finish and an exposed anchor position.

This route fully deserves its popularity and offers a great warm-up option for the harder routes around it. Expect the route to have parties on it, or waiting, on busy days. However, if you have to wait for a chance to get on it, don't be discouraged - it's well worth the wait.

Slander Sector

- 163 Bitter Has Been 12a ★★
- 164 Slander Magnet 12b ★★★
- 165 Slander Up 12a ★★★
- 166 All Washed Up 11d ★★★
- 167 Baby Face 10b ★★
- 168 The Forgotten 12c ★★
- 169 Defamation 11c ★★
- 170 Drama 11a ★★
- 171 Fueled by Slander 11c ★★★
- 172 Mudslinger 11d ★
- 173 Shockwave 10d ★★★
- 174 Aftershock 11a ★★

Slander Sector

This sector is found just to the right of the Torture Machine Area, and right of the top of the main climber's trail. There are a number of good routes found here, including: *Shockwave* (10d), *Fueled by Slander* (11c), *All Washed Up* (11d), and *Slander Magnet* (12b).

The routes are described left to right.

163 Bitter Has Been 12a ★★ ❑
12 bolts to a double ring anchor, 29m/95'. Start climbing twenty feet right of *Vertigo* and follow the left-trending ramp. After clipping the second bolt, climb straight of the jutting arête and over the bulge. Easier climbing after the bulge leads the a final bulge at the top of the route. FA: Louie Anderson 2005.

164 Slander Magnet 12b ★★★ ❑
10 bolts to a double ring anchor, 27m/90'. This route starts ten feet right of *Bitter Has Been* and climbs broken terrain to a smooth face. After clipping the fourth bolt traverse up and left before climbing through the upper bulge. FA: Louie Anderson

165 Slander Up 12a ★★★ ❑
10 bolts to a double ring anchor, 27m/90'. A link–up. Begin as for *Slander Magnet*, but after clipping the fourth bolt move up and right (passing one independent bolt) to join *All Washed Up* at its seventh bolt. FA: Louie Anderson 2005.

166 All Washed Up 11d ★★★ ❑
11 bolts to a double ring anchor, 27m/90'. Start just right of *Slander Magnet* and climb past a pair of sloping ledges. Continue on fun climbing (mainly using large features) to the anchors. FA: Louie Anderson 2005.

167 Baby Face 10b ★★ ❑
7 bolts to a double ring anchor, 21m,70'. Starting fifteen feet right of *All Washed Up*, climb left up a ramp to the first bolt. After moving through a small bulge follow big, blocky features to the anchors. FA: Louie Anderson 2005.

168 The Forgotten 12c ★★ ❑
10 bolts a double ring anchor, 24m/80'. Begin climbing six feet right of *Baby Face* at a right-facing flake. Climb up the left side of this flake and after clipping the second bolt, move left to an undercling crux. Continue straight up and after clipping the sixth bolt, move right to join *Defamation* at its sixth bolt. Finish on that route. FA: Louie Anderson 2009.

169 Defamation 11c ★★ ❑
9 bolts to a double ring anchor, 24m/80'. This route starts just right of *The Forgotten*. After clipping the first bolt move straight up, past a powerful throw, to finish up the easier, but unique stepped ledge system above. FA: Louie Anderson 2005.

Slander Sector

170 Drama 11a ★★ ☐
7 bolts to a double ring anchor, 21m/70'. Begin climbing up the juggy slab eight feet right of the arête, before dealing with the steep and sequential corner above. FA: Louie Anderson 2006.

171 Fueled by Slander 11c ★★★ ☐
11 bolts to a double ring anchor, 29m/95'. Climb the middle of the face (right of the seam). A long and varied route that is one of the most popular on this section of cliff. FA: Louie Anderson 2005.

172 Mudslinger 11d ★ ☐
8 bolts to a double ring anchor, 27m/90'. Start just left of the right arête and climb up to and over a small roof. Continue up the dihedral above. FA: Louie Anderson 2005.

173 Shockwave 10d ★★★ ☐
8 bolts to a double ring anchor, 26m/85'. Located around the corner from *Mudslinger*. Climb the face just right of the arête. After clipping the third bolt, move right and follow the big flakes before moving back left to finish. FA: Louie Anderson 2005.

174 Aftershock 11a ★★ ☐
9 bolts to a double ring anchor, 26m/85'. This route starts eight feet right of *Shockwave* and climbs up to a large, obvious flake. A crux getting onto the sloping shelf above this flake leads to a series of steep, left-facing flakes and liebacks. FA: Louie Anderson 2007.

Alice Rietveld on Torture Machine (12b)

Rubble Row

- 175 Playing with Fire 13a ★★
- 176 Disco Inferno 10c ★
- 177 Flake and Bake 5.8 ★
- 178 Burnout 11c ★
- 179 Victim of Reality 10a ★★
- 180 Prisoner of Society 10b ★★
- 181 Sika Soldier 12c ★
- 182 Energy Crisis 13a ★★★
- 183 Energy King 13b ★★★★
- 184 King Pin 13a ★★★★★
- 185 Fiasco 11c ★
- 186 Choss Toss 13b ★★
- 187 Jaunt 10b ★★
- 188 The Plague 10d ★★
- 189 Tailspin 10a ★★
- 190 The Lowdown 10b ★★
- 191 Loopfrog 5.9 ★★
- 192 Lowrider 10b ★

Climber's Guide: Riverside Quarry • 113

Rubble Row

Rubble Row is located just to the right of the Slander Sector. The routes in this area are primarily shorter than those found on the other Quarry walls. They also climb somewhat lesser quality rock. They have however cleaned up, and will continue to do so with more traffic. The area was primarily developed to offer additional moderate route options to the local climbing community, and some fun routes were the result, as well as some surprising good harder routes. The better routes in this area include: *Leapfrog* (5.9), *Victim of Reality* (10a), *The Plague* (10d), and the amazing *King Pin* (13a).

The routes are described left to right.

175 Playing with Fire 13a ★★ ❑

6 bolts to a double ring anchor, 14m/45'. This route starts at the left edge of the sloped shelf. Climb up a faint seam to reach a left-facing corner system. Better rock and harder than it appears. A short and savage route. FA: Louie Anderson 2008.

176 Disco Inferno 10c ★ ❑

7 bolts to a double ring anchor, 14m/45'. Begin climbing six feet right of *Playing with Fire* and climb up and right, before moving back left and following a faint seam in a corner. Fun climbing on positive holds leads to anchors on the ledge above. FA: Louie Anderson 2008.

177 Flake and Bake 5.8 ★ ❑

7 bolts to a double ring anchor, 15m/50'. Starts thirty feet downhill from *Disco Inferno* right off the climber's trail. A short steep section leads to ledges and the obvious left-facing flake. Follow the flake as it curves around to the right, ultimately finishing up a short slabby section. FA: Louie Anderson 2007.

178 Burnout 11c ★ ❑

8 bolts to a double ring anchor, 16m/55'. This route starts six feet right of *Flake and Bake* and climbs straight up, following the right side of a pair of seams. Shares the anchors of *Flake and Bake*. FA: Louie Anderson 2008.

179 Victim of Reality 10a ★★ ❑

9 bolts to a double ring anchor, 20m,65'. Begin climbing eight feet right of *Burnout* and climb straight up to a shallow overlap at the second bolt. Continue up and right and climb around the right side of the upper bulge, before finishing at anchors on the slab above. FA: Louie Anderson 2008.

180 Prisoner of Society 10b ★★ ❑

9 bolts a double ring anchor, 21m/70'. This route starts directly in front of the bench, ten feet right of *Victim of Reality,* where a large flake is lying against the base of the wall. Climb the edge-filled slab above to reach underclings moving up and left at the fifth bolt. Finishes at shared anchors with *Victim of Reality*. FA: Louie Anderson 2008.

Rubble Row

⑱ Sika Soldier 12c ★ ☐

11 bolts to a double ring anchor, 30m/100'. This and the following routes climb the obvious tower located thirty-five feet downhill and to the right of *Prisoner of Society*. Starts at the bottom of the staircase and follows the leftmost line of bolts. After clipping the first bolt, move up and left following a stepped ledge. Continue following bolts up to and over a small roof at mid-height, and then trending up and right along a flake. Finish up the depression to high anchors. An impressive looking line that is unfortunately plagued by inferior rock quality. FA: Louie Anderson 2007.

⑱ Energy Crisis 13a ★★★ ☐

10 bolts to a double ring anchor, 30m/100'. Begin as for *Sika Soldier,* but after clipping the first bolt, continue straight up following a faint seam and blocky features high in the route. FA: Louie Anderson 2007.

⑱ Energy King 13b ★★★★ ☐

11 bolts to a double ring anchor, 30m/100'. A link up. Climb *Energy Crisis* to its fourth bolt, before moving right to join *King Pin* at its fifth bolt. Finish on that route. Includes the hardest parts of both routes. FA: Louie Anderson 2007.

⑱ King Pin 13a ★★★★★ ☐

11 bolts to a double ring anchor, 30m/100'. Arguably the best 5.13 at the crag. This Quarry classic starts five feet right of *Energy Crisis* and climbs straight up the front, right side of the thin pillar. Powerful and steep moves low lead to thin finger cracks in the middle of the route. The technical crux follows, passing over a shallow overlap, before dealing with the devious move to the finger lock. Finishes around the block at the top of the tower. FA: Louie Anderson 2006.

⑱ Fiasco 11c ★ ☐

7 bolts to a double ring anchor, 15m/50'. This route starts eight feet right of *King Pin* and climbs a short powerful face, finishing up easier terrain, more or less following a very faint seam After clipping the sixth bolt, move up and right to finish at the anchors on the face of the short pillar. FA: Louie Anderson 2007.

⑱ Choss Toss 13b ★★ ☐

14 bolts to a double ring anchor, 30m/100'. Climb *Fiasco* and after clipping that route's sixth bolt, climb up and left to reach the steep left wall. Follow the flake on that wall before moving left on crimps high on the route, to finish at the left arête. FA: Louie Anderson 2007.

⑱ Jaunt 10b ★★ ☐

6 bolts to a double ring anchor, 15m/50'. Begin climbing eight feet right of *Fiasco,* at the right edge of the face. Climb straight up and after clipping the second bolt, move left to join and finish on *Fiasco*. FA: Louie Anderson 2007.

⑱ The Plague 10d ★★ ☐

7 bolts to a double ring anchor, 15m/50'. Just a few feet right of *Jaunt,* climb straight up and follow the crack system. FA: Louie Anderson 2007.

Rubble Row • Route Profile

King Pin
ROUTE PROFILE

Climber: Leah Sandvoss *Photos: Andre Kiryanov*

Rubble Row • Route Profile

184 King Pin 13a ★★★★★

For complete route description see page 115

"This route represents everything I like about the Quarry...it really has it all...thin moves down low, sustained climbing with a somewhat technical crux at the mid-point and then the redpoint crux...including hand jams and finger locks...it's a route regardless of pure strength that can still spit you off time and time again..."

Nino Guagliano

Perhaps the best hard route at the Quarry – and that's saying something, given the number of high-quality hard routes to be found here. The fact that this lone pillar of good rock is surrounded by huge expanses of lesser quality rock makes it that much more valuable in contrast.

Somewhat thuggy moves down low lead to an optional rest out right. This is followed by a short crack section and the most prominent bulge on the route at mid-height. A devious crux here deposits the climber at a committing move to a perfect finger lock. The block just prior to the anchors provides the final challenge. As Nino alludes to above, the successful redpointer needs a full bag of tricks to succeed.

Removed from the more travelled sections of the cliff, but well worth the walk. In fact the comparable solitude of the route's location is a nice break from the more popular areas of the cliff.

Rubble Row

Matt Callender on Nostalgia (11c)

Rubble Row

189 Tailspin 10a ★★ ❏

7 bolts to a double ring anchor, 15m/50'. Begin as for *The Plague*, but after clipping that route's first bolt, move up and right into the corner right of the pillar. After clipping the fourth bolt, move up and left to join and finish on *The Plague*. You can also finish at the anchors of *The Lowdown* by climbing up and right after clipping the fourth bolt. FA: Louie Anderson 2007.

190 The Lowdown 10b ★★ ❏

7 bolts to a double ring anchor, 12m/40'. This route starts eight feet right of *Tailspin* on the right side of the large boulder on the ground. Climb the blunt prow, moving up and left after clipping the second bolt. Follow the high, right-facing dihedral to the anchors. FA: Louie Anderson 2007.

191 Leapfrog 5.9 ★★ ❏

7 bolts to a double ring anchor, 15m/50'. Starts about ten feet downhill from *The Lowdown*, off the low ledge. Climb straight up, passing a large flake between the second and third bolts. Follow a left-facing, shallow dihedral and, after clipping the sixth bolt, move up and right to the last bolt, before stepping right to the anchors of *Lowrider*. Alternately, you can finish up and left to join *The Lowdown* at its fourth bolt and finish for that route. FA: Louie Anderson 2007.

192 Lowrider 10b ★ ❏

7 bolts to a double ring anchor 15m/50'. Begin climbing from the right end of the same ledge where *Leapfrog* begins. Clip the right bolt and climb up and right, following the obvious dihedral and clipping bolts on the right wall. FA: Louie Anderson 2007.

Felix Casanova on Kingpin (13a)

Slide Zone

120 • Climber's Guide: Riverside Quarry

Slide Zone

- (193) **Lowrider Direct 10b** ★★
- (194) **Power Surge 12b** ★★★
- (195) **Mud Monster 14b/c** ★★★★
- (196) **All That Remains 12d** ★★★★
- (197) **Tiptoe 5.7** ★★
- (198) **Point Blank 13a** ★★
- (199) **Funk Flake 12b** ★★
- (200) **Beautiful Disaster 12d** ★★★★
- (201) **Alpha Male 13a** ★★★
- (202) **Mud Ramp 10a** ★★
- (203) **Alpha Dog 13a** ★★★
- (204) **Cruiser 10d** ★
- (205) **Supercruiser 12c** ★★★

Found just to the right of Rubble Row, and running downhill, this section of cliff brackets the point where the top of the talus slopes back down to ground level. There are a number of steep faces located in this area, including a northwest facing series of tiered, white faces. There are some easier slabs on the lower portion of the wall, and some high quality harder routes on the upper expanses of rock. The standout routes are *Mud Ramp* (10a), *Power Surge* (12b), *Funk Flake* (12b), *All That Remains* (12d), *Beautiful Disaster* (12d), and the unclimbed *Mud Monster* (14b/c).

All routes start on the lower level and are described left to right.

(193) Lowrider Direct 10b ★★ ❏

10 bolts to a double ring anchor, 24m/80'. This route climbs the furthest left lines of bolts going up the clean slab. After clipping the fifth bolt, continue up and left to join *Lowrider* at its third bolt. Finish up that route's corner system. FA: Louie Anderson 2009.

(194) Power Surge 12b ★★★ ❏

10 bolts to a double ring anchor, 23m/75'. Begin as for *Lowrider Direct*, but after clipping the fifth bolt, move up and right onto the steep face. Powerful, and sometimes big, moves lead to anchors on the ledge above the short face. FA: Louie Anderson 2008.

(195) Mud Monster 14b/c ★★★★ ❏

OPEN PROJECT 25 bolts to a double ring anchor, **48m/160' – lower to anchors of #188 The Plague with a 70-meter rope.** Perhaps the most impressive looking line in the Quarry. If the rock quality were better, this would be a nationally known route and have the full 5-star quality rating. As it is, it is still worthy of attention for those that can climb the grade. Begin this route by climbing *Power Surge*. After reaching the ledge at the end of that route, do not clip its anchors, but instead continue straight up, clipping two additional bolts, before moving up and left along the steep, diagonalling face. Very sustained climbing with minimal rests leads up the long face. OB: Louie Anderson 2008. FA: None yet – open project.

Slide Zone

196 All That Remains 12d ★★★★ ☐

18 bolts to a double ring anchor, **36m/120' – lower with a 70-meter rope.** Climb *Power Surge*, but instead of clipping that route's anchors, continue straight up the wall above the ledge. A high, technical crux at the upper bulge baffles many climbers. FA: Louie Anderson 2008.

197 Tiptoe 5.7 ★★ ☐

5 bolts to a double ring anchor, 12m/40'. This route climbs the center of the slab, just right of *Lowrider Direct*. Route ends at anchors below the obvious large, right-facing flake. FA: Louie Anderson 2009.

198 Point Blank 13a ★★ ☐

11 bolts to a double ring anchor, 24m,80'. Climb *Tiptoe* and at the end of that route, continue up the obvious hanging flake. After clipping the second bolt on the flake, move left diagonally across the steep face. Finishes at the anchors of *Power Surge*. FA: Louie Anderson 2008.

199 Funk Flake 12b ★★ ☐

11 bolts to a double ring anchor, 24m/80'. Climb *Point Blank*, but instead of climbing left onto the face after the eighth bolt, continue straight up the flake to anchors at its top ledge. FA: Louie Anderson 2008.

200 Beautiful Disaster 12d ★★★★ ☐

20 bolts to a double ring anchor, **36m/120' – lower with a 70-meter rope.** Climb *Funk Flake*, but instead of clipping that route's anchors, move right and climb another right-facing flake system on the edge of the face. Continue over stepped overlaps on the face above. FA: Louie Anderson 2008.

201 Alpha Male 13a ★★★ ☐

18 bolts to a double ring anchor, **36m/120' – lower with a 70-meter rope.** Climb *Tiptoe* and after clipping its fifth bolt, move up and right, clipping the last bolt of *Mud Ramp*, and continuing onto the steep face. After clipping the ninth bolt, climb straight up the steep face, right of the arête, past several overlaps. FA: Louie Anderson 2008.

202 Mud Ramp 10a ★★ ☐

9 bolts to a double ring anchor, 20m/65'. This route begins twelve feet downhill from *Tiptoe* and climbs the short arête at the right side of the face. When you reach the top of the arête, trend up and left, diagonally following the ramp to the anchors of *Tiptoe*. FA: Louie Anderson 2008.

203 Alpha Dog 13a ★★★ ☐

20 bolts to a double ring anchor, **36m/120' – lower with a 70-meter rope.** Climb *Mud Ramp*, but after clipping the sixth bolt, move up and right onto the steep face to join and finish on *Alpha Male*. FA: Louie Anderson 2008.

204 Cruiser 10d ★ ☐

8 bolts to a double ring anchor, 16m/55'. Begin climbing six feet right of *Mud Ramp*. Follow the faint seam at the base up and right through a series of overlaps. Continue straight up the wall to anchors in a depressed ledge, halfway up the wall. FA: Louie Anderson 2005.

Slide Zone

Brian Cullen high on Supercruiser (12c)

205 Supercruiser 12c ★★★ ☐

15 bolts to a double ring anchor, 36m/120' – lower with a 70-meter rope. Climb *Cruiser*, but after clipping that route's anchors continue up and right onto the steep face. Challenging moves lead over multiple bulges. FA: Louie Anderson 2005.

The Tall Wall

The Tall Wall

206 Gravitational Attraction
12b ★★★

207 American Idiot
12c ★★★★

208 Silver Streaker
12a ★★★

209 The World Below
12a ★★★★

210 Lucky
12a ★★★★

The Tall Wall

The Tall Wall is found just right of the Slide Zone at ground level. Its base is located behind a collection of large boulders, at the top of a low talus field. These boulders are home to some established boulder problems, and still have room for more development on the steep left side of the leftmost boulder. This wall is home to some of the longest pitches at the crag, including the longest: *Silver Streaker* (12a). All of the routes are highly recommended.

The routes are described left to right.

206 Gravitational Attraction 12b ★★★ ❏

21 bolts to a double ring anchor, **42m/140' L-P-L.** This route begins near the left edge of the face and pulls over a low, powerful bulge. After the bulge, follow a series of right-facing corners and flakes. After passing a ledge at the eighth bolt, continue straight up, more or less following a thin seam. Ultimately, climb the face left of the right-facing dihedral. FA: Louie Anderson 2005.

207 American Idiot 12c ★★★★ ❏

19 bolts to a double ring anchor, **42m/140' L-P-L using 100' anchors of** *Gravitational Attraction.* Begin six feet to the right of *Gravitational Attraction* and climb up and over the right side of the same low bulge. Continue up the center of the face and follow the left-facing flake to underclings, before moving right and climbing the center of the wall to shared anchors with *Gravitational Attraction.* FA: Louie Anderson 2005.

208 Silver Streaker 12a ★★★ ❏

24 bolts to a double ring anchor, **53m/175' L-P-L cautiously using a 70-meter rope.** This is the longest single pitch in the Quarry and starts twelve feet right of *American Idiot* at the obvious right-facing flake. Climb past this and continue past a series of flakes before crossing a ledge at the seventh bolt. Continue up the face above, eventually finishing up the drill flute at the top of the cliff. FA: Brent Webster 2005.

209 The World Below 12a ★★★★ ❏

18 bolts to a double ring anchor, **39m/130' – lower with a 70-meter rope.** This route begins about ten feet right of *Silver Streaker,* just right of the obvious drill flute. Climb the face on predominantly positive edges and flakes to high anchors. Caution: **Rope stretcher to lower with a 70-meter rope.** FA: Louie Anderson 2008.

210 Lucky 12a ★★★★ ❏

12 bolts to 2 open shuts, 30m/100'. Begin climbing off the upper, right platform. Lean around the arête to clip the first bolt prior to starting. Classic granite climbing, following big edges, flakes and ramps, with a definite technical crux high on the route. FA: Louie Anderson 2004.

The Shield

126 • Climber's Guide: Riverside Quarry

The Shield

- (211) Redneck Agenda 12b ★★★★
- (212) The Enemy Within 12b ★★★
- (213) Force Fed 11d ★★
- (214) Enigma 13b ★★★★★
- (215) Tattoo 13b ★★★
- (216) Gypsy 13c ★★★★★
- (217) Divine Intervention 12b ★★★
- (218) Headstrong 13a ★★★
- (219) Control Freak 13a ★★★
- (220) Power Junkie 13a ★★★★
- (221) Megalomania 12a ★★★★★
- (222) Redneck Reality 12b ★★★★
- (223) Block Party 12a ★★★

The Shield is located just to the right of The Tall Wall, on top of a small talus platform, and is identified by a large, smooth section of rock. The routes found on *The Shield* are noticeably more technical in nature than those found elsewhere at the crag. Further, almost every route here is popular, clean and high quality. The comfortable base area is an added bonus. Standout routes of this area include *Megalomania* (12a), *The Enemy Within* (12b), *Redneck Reality* (12b), *Enigma* (13b), and *Gypsy* (13c). This area has one of the highest concentrations of difficult climbing found at the crag.

Routes are described from left to right.

(211) Redneck Agenda 12b ★★★★ ☐

12 bolts to 2 open shuts, 30m/100'. A link-up. Climb *The Enemy Within* to its seventh bolts before moving left to join *Lucky* at its eighth bolt. Finish up that route. A great combination of the two routes, offering the cruxes of both. FA: Louie Anderson 2004.

(212) The Enemy Within 12b ★★★ ☐

12 bolts to 2 open shuts, 30m/100'. Climb the obvious dihedral and then continue through the bulge above via a committing deadpoint. Finishes up the sustained headwall on a series of flake systems. FA: Louie Anderson 2004.

(213) Force Fed 11d ★★ ☐

5 bolts to 2 open shuts, 12m/40'. Begin climbing eight feet right of the dihedral and pull through several small bulges. An action packed and somewhat popular warm-up for the longer routes on the wall. FA: Louie Anderson 2004.

The Shield • Route Profile

Enigma
ROUTE PROFILE

Climber: Chris Lindner

The Shield • Route Profile

214 Enigma 13b ★★★★★

For complete route description see page 130

All three of the routes on this panel of rock are among the best hard pitches found at the Quarry. They are also some of the most technically challenging. While not the hardest of the three, Enigma was the most mentioned when the climber surveys were performed to determine which routes should be profiled.

This route climbs the left edge of the blank-looking shield of rock that is one of the cleanest pieces of stone at the crag. Very bouldery, very crimpy, and very sequential climbing on the lower half of the climb, thankfully leads to easier climbing on the top half. Were the entire route as sustained as the bottom, this quality line would be far more difficult.

While the two routes to the right do have some manufactured holds, Enigma is all natural. Glue has been used to reinforce some of the thin crimps on the climb, but they are all as they were found when the line was first bolted. Originally, this climb was rated more difficult, and climbed a more direct sequence through its crux. When working on the second ascent, Chris Lindner found a previously unused side pull feature a little to the left of the original line of climbing. This new feature provided a welcome rest in the middle of the difficult climbing and has become the adopted sequence for the climb's main challenge.

Enigma is a beautiful climb, which offers a technically demanding challenge, and should be a goal for any 5.13 climber.

The Shield

Elke Lindner on Tattoo (13b)

㉔ Enigma 13b ★★★★★ ❏

12 bolts to 2 open shuts, 30m/100'. This excellent route starts at the left edge of a low roof. Begin climbing off the top of the large boulder. A crimpy face leads to an undercling at the second bolt. After clipping this bolt, climb through the initial bulge and continue up the clean and crimpy face above. After the mid-height crux, still challenging moves lead to the anchor. FA: Louie Anderson 2004.

㉕ Tattoo 13b ★★★ ❏

15 bolts to a double chain anchor, 30m/100'. Start climbing twelve feet right of *Enigma,* behind the large boulder. Climb up to the first bolt in a shallow corner and continue through the short, steep headwall above. After pulling the lower bulge, continuous edge climbing leads to a final challenge high on the route. OB: Grahm Doe FA: Louie Anderson 2004.

㉖ Gypsy 13c ★★★★★ ❏

14 bolts to double chain anchor, 30m/100'. Begin fifteen feet right of *Tattoo,* directly behind the smaller boulder. Climb up to and over a small overlap and continue on the clean face above using sequential moves before finishing on easier, but still challenging, climbing. Precise footwork is the key to success on this one. OB: Grahm Doe FA: Brent Webster 2004.

㉗ Divine Intervention 12b ★★★ ❏

14 bolts to a double chain anchor, 30m/100'. This route starts just right of *Gypsy.* Climb over a small bulge and follow the blunt prow above. After clipping the tenth bolt, move left to join *Gypsy* at its twelfth bolt. FA: Louie Anderson 2006.

㉘ Headstrong 13a ★★★ ❏

13 bolts to a double ring anchor, 30m/100'. A link-up. Start as for *Control Freak,* but after clipping that route's eighth bolt move up and left, clipping two independent bolts, before joining Gypsy at its eleventh bolt. Finish up that route. FA: Louie Anderson 2004.

The Shield

㉑⑨ Control Freak 13a ★★★ ❏

10 bolts to 2 open shuts, 30m/100'. This route starts just right of the low roof. Initially positive holds lead to thinner and thinner climbing until you are ultimately faced with the deadpoint crux. Finishes up a smooth, steep headwall on blocky jugs. FA: Louie Anderson 2004.

㉒⓪ Power Junkie 13a ★★★★ ❏

12 bolts to 2 open shuts, 30m/100'. A link-up. Start as for *Control Freak*, but after clipping the seventh bolt move right past one independent bolt to join *Megalomania* at it's ninth bolt. FA: Louie Anderson 2004.

㉒① Megalomania 12a ★★★★★ ❏

12 bolts to 2 open shuts, 30m/100'. A nice long endurance challenge that starts six feet right of *Control Freak*. Clean rock and interesting movement lead to a long arête and corner system. If you want full value, don't be tempted by the rests off to the right in the middle of the route. For those wanting to lessen the challenge further, it's become common for many climbers to avoid the upper crux by climbing up and left after clipping the ninth bolt and finishing at the anchors of *Control Freak*. While still a nice route, those doing so are missing quite a lot higher up. FA: Louie Anderson 2004.

㉒② Redneck Reality 12b ★★★★ ❏

14 bolts to a double ring anchor, 27m/90'. This route starts fifteen feet right of *Megalomania* at a thin, curved edge and flake. Climb up and slightly left before dealing with a series of bulges. Good rests after each bulge preserve your strength for the final, steep challenge. FA: Louie Anderson 2005

㉒③ Block Party 12a ★★★ ❏

14 bolts to a double ring anchor, 30m/100' Found ten feet right of *Redneck Reality,* this route climbs right-facing, blocky features up to and over a high headwall. FA: Louie Anderson 2005.

Tom Lindner on Gypsy (13c)

Anger Management Area

132 • Climber's Guide: Riverside Quarry

Anger Management Area

- **224** Block Suppression 12a ★★★
- **225** Aggression Suppression 12c ★★★
- **226** Anger Management 12b ★★★★
- **227** Infatuation 12b ★★★★
- **228** Exfoliator 11c ★★★★
- **229** Spunky Monkey 11c ★★★
- **230** Spunk 12a ★★★
- **231** Afterburner 11c ★★
- **232** Shiver Giver 12b ★★★
- **233** Vascular Massacre 11b ★★★★
- **234** Vascular Funk 11d ★★★
- **235** Funkadelic 12c ★★★

This area is found directly to the right of The Shield. The rock here is more featured than that area, and the routes require a good blend of technical ability and general fitness to succeed on. There are many more moderate classics to be found, including: *Vascular Massacre* (11b), *Exfoliator* (11c), *Anger Management* (12b), *and Shiver Giver* (12b).

Routes are described from left to right.

224 Block Suppression 12a ★★★ ☐

15 bolts to a double ring anchor, 30m/100'. A link up. Climb *Block Party* to its fourth bolt and then climb up and right to join *Aggression Suppression* at its fourth bolt. Finish on that route. FA: Louie Anderson 2007.

225 Aggression Suppression 12c ★★★ ☐

14 bolts to a double ring anchor, 30m/100'. This route starts ten feet right of *Block Party*. A hard boulder problem leads to a big left-facing side pull. Continue over the shallow bulges above before moving right after clipping the eleventh bolt to join *Anger Management* at its twelfth bolt. Route can be extended by climbing to the second set of anchors on *Anger Management*. Descend as for that route. FA: Louie Anderson 2007.

226 Anger Management 12b ★★★★ ☐

19 bolts to a double ring anchor, 45m/150' L-P-L. Starts 35 feet right of *Megalomania*. Climb up to a long, arched undercling flake. Fun climbing on edges leads to the first bulge. The powerful climbing at the second bulge provides the pump that keeps the easier climbing above challenging. The top holds will sometimes get a dusting of sand after heavy rain storms. There is usually a pile of cheat stones at the start of the climb. FA: Brent Webster 2004.

Anger Management Area

Brent Webster on Exfoliator (11c)

Anger Management Area

㉗ Infatuation 12b ★★★★ ☐

15 bolts to a double ring anchor, 30m/100'. A link-up. Climb *Exfoliator* to its first bolt and then continue up the right-facing arête feature and face above. Once you reach the left-trending dihedral, climb up and left to join *Anger Management* at its tenth bolt. Route can be extended by climbing to the second set of anchors on *Anger Management*. Descend as for that route. FA: Louie Anderson 2008.

㉘ Exfoliator 11c ★★★★ ☐

11 bolts to 2 open shuts, 30m/100'. 8 feet right of *Anger Management* is a left-facing flake. Climb this to its end before traversing right to the arête. Steep moves lead to a long right-facing system of flakes and fins. After passing over a bulge at the end of this system, enjoy the rest before the final section of steep climbing. Good to the last move. FA: Louie Anderson 2004.

㉙ Spunky Monkey 11c ★★★ ☐

10 bolts to 2 open shuts, 30m/100'. Begin climbing 10 feet right of *Exfoliator*. Climb the awkward corner system then up and slightly right through the blocky terrain above. Continue up the right of two shallow flake/ramp systems to the sixth bolt. After clipping this move left to join *Exfoliator* at its eighth bolt. FA: Louie Anderson 2004.

㉚ Spunk 12a ★★★ ☐

12 bolts to a double ring anchor, 30m/100'. Begin as for *Spunky Monkey*, but after clipping the sixth bolt continue up and right into the right-facing dihedral. FA: Louie Anderson 2006

㉛ Afterburner 11c ★★ ☐

12 bolts to a double ring anchor, 30m/100'. Starts six feet right of *Spunk* and climbs the big, right-facing dihedral up to and over a final bulge. FA: Louie Anderson 2006.

㉜ Shiver Giver 12b ★★★ ☐

13 bolts to a double ring anchor, 30m/100'. Climb the light-colored face ten feet right of *Afterburner*. The initial smooth face leads to a series of bulges. FA: Louie Anderson 2006.

㉝ Vascular Massacre 11b ★★★★ ☐

11 bolts to a double ring anchor, 27m/90'. This route starts eighteen feet right of *Shiver Giver*. Begin on the reinforced section of trail and climb up and left following big, blocky features. The upper portion of the route follows the obvious corner system until the crux bulge at the end of the route. This route can be very pumpy. FA: Louie Anderson 2006.

㉞ Vascular Funk 11d ★★★ ☐

12 bolts to a double ring anchor, 27m/90'. A link up. Begin by climbing *Vascular Massacre*, but after clipping that route's eighth bolt, move up and right past an independent bolt, before joining *Funkadelic* at its ninth bolt. Climb the upper crux of and finish on that route. FA: Louie Anderson 2011.

Anger Management Area

Eric Erikson on Spunk (12a)

Anger Management Area

235 Funkadelic 12c ★★★ ❑

11 bolts to a double ring anchor, 27m/90'. Start climbing just right of *Vascular Massacre* and follow a shallow, right-facing corner to a sloping ledge system. A short headwall leads to a dished rest and the steep, upper face. Sequential and powerful. FA: Louie Anderson 2006.

Ronnie Jenkins on Megalomania (12a)

Taboo Area

138 • Climber's Guide: Riverside Quarry

Taboo Area

- (236) Spitfire 12b ★
- (237) Scorched Earth 12b ★★
- (238) No Man's Land 12b ★★★
- (239) Mission Possible 13c ★★★★★
- (240) The Saint 13a ★★★★★
- (241) Chris Cross 13b ★★★★
- (242) Fusion 14b ★★★★★
- (243) Wages of Sin 12c ★★★
- (244) Sins of the Flesh 13a ★★★
- (245) Original Sin 11b ★★★
- (246) The Sinner 13a ★★★
- (247) Open Project 5.15 ?
- (248) Taboo 12c ★★★★★
- (249) Sky Pilot 12c ★★★★★
- (250) Violator 11c ★★★★★
- (251) Wicked Violator 5.13b ★★★★
- (252) Lothario 13c ★★★★
- (253) Seduction 12d ★★★★
- (254) Seduction Supreme 13c ★★★★
- (255) Temptation 12d ★★★
- (256) Temptation Supreme 13d ★★★★★
- (257) Forbidden Fruit 12a ★★★★★
- (258) Magic Mushroom 11b ★★★
- (259) Handful of Harpies 11c ★★
- (260) First Born 13b ★★★
- (261) Cavorting 10d ★★
- (262) Run Amok 11b ★★★
- (263) Purple Haze 12b ★★★
- (264) Solidarity 12b ★★★★
- (265) Runaway 12a ★★★
- (266) Momentum 12b ★★★★
- (267) Rocky 11d ★★★

This was the first area to see renewed sport climbing interest and the quality of the routes found here are what kept the developers interested in continuing their efforts. There are several good climbs to be found here, but the standouts are *Violator* (11c), *Forbidden Fruit* (12a), *Taboo* (12c), *The Saint* (13a) and *Temptation Supreme* (13d).

Routes are described left to right.

(236) Spitfire 12b ★ ☐

 6 bolts to a double ring anchor, 16m/55'. This route begins climbing at the top of the steps that lead down to the Anger Management Area. Start just left of the arête and climb up the featured slab. Above the ledge, finish up the dihedral above. Awkward and harder than it looks. FA: Louie Anderson 2005.

(237) Scorched Earth 12b ★★ ☐

7 bolts to 2 open shuts, 16m/55'. A technical outing that climbs the big, stemming corner at the far left of the face to a high crux. FA: Louie Anderson 2003.

Taboo Area

(238) No Man's Land 12b ★★★ ❏

12 bolts to 2 open shuts, 30m/100'. Climb a series of left-facing flakes to a rest at mid-route. From here climb past several flat shelves and bulges to a final crimpy section. FA: Louie Anderson 2003.

(239) Mission Possible 13c ★★★★★ ❏

13 bolts to a double ring anchor, 30m/100'. This route begins eight feet right of *No Man's Land* on small crimps, just below a featured undercling flake. A boulder problem off the ground leads to positive holds at the first clip. Climb straight up the face, passing over shallow bulges. After clipping the seventh bolt, join *No Man's Land* at its ninth bolt. Clip this bolt and two more, before climbing straight up through the steep headwall, passing another three bolts. A high boulder problem provides the redpoint challenge. OB: Louie Anderson. FA: Chris Lindner 2006.

(240) The Saint 13a ★★★★★ ❏

13 bolts to a double biner anchor, 30m/100'. Begin climbing just right of *Mission Possible* at a diagonal seam. Powerful moves on the bottom half lead to a steeper and more difficult upper half. A great route that would only be better if the middle were more difficult. FA: Grahm Doe 2003.

(241) Chris Cross 13b ★★★★ ❏

8 bolts to a double chain anchor, 14m/45'. A direct start to *Wages of Sin*. Start climbing at the left edge of the gold streaks. Very thin crimps and side pulls lead to a shelf deadpoint. Continue up and right to join *Wages of Sin* at its sixth bolt. OB: Louie Anderson 2003. FA: Chris Lindner 2005.

(242) Fusion 14b ★★★★★ ❏

17 bolts to a double ring anchor, 30m/100'. Climb *Criss Cross,* but instead of clipping the anchors of that route, continue up the steep upper face, through the high bulge. Technical moves with a low-percentage crux at the top of the climb. Currently the hardest route at the crag. FA: Louie Anderson 2005.

(243) Wages of Sin 12c ★★★ ❏

8 bolts to a double chain anchor, 15m/50'. Start climbing at the far left edge of a narrow ledge. Follow a vertical seam over a very small roof. After clipping the second bolt move left following clean crimps to a small right-facing corner. From here a series of flakes and seams lead to a short traverse right to the anchors. FA: Louie Anderson 2003.

(244) Sins of the Flesh 13a ★★★ ❏

6 bolts to a double chain anchor, 14m/45'. Start as for *Wages of Sin,* but after clipping the second bolt continue up and slightly right. Smooth rock and small holds present the challenge on this technical line. Finish at anchors of *Original Sin*. FA: Louie Anderson 2003.

(245) Original Sin 11b ★★★ ❏

6 bolts to a double chain anchor, 14m/45'. The best pockets you'll ever see in granite lead up this steep line. Enjoyable, gymnastic moves lead up the blunt arête, before moving left to climb the short, clean headwall. It possible to climb up and left past another bolt to reach anchors on a ledge, and to use this route as an approach pitch for *Taboo*. FA: Mark Maynard 1992.

Taboo Area

(246) The Sinner 13a ★★★ ❏

6 bolts to a double biner anchor, 18m/60'. From the ledge anchors traverse up and left (clipping one independent bolt) to join and finish on *The Saint*. A shortcut into that route's hard, upper crux. FA: Louie Anderson 2003.

(247) Open Project 5.15 ? ❏

8 bolts to two Metolius Rap Hangers, 18m/60'. This route starts off the ledge above *Wages of Sin*, and climbs the steep face between *Fusion* and *Taboo* on manufactured holds. EB: Louie Anderson 2005

(248) Taboo 12c ★★★★★ ❏

2 bolts, nuts and cams to 1", 18m/60. Located above *Original Sin*. From the ledge anchors follow bolts up and right through bulges to the base of a very clean dihedral. A finger sized crack gets thinner and the walls get steeper as you get higher on this classic route. Brilliant! FA: (aid) Unknown. FFA: Louie Anderson 2003.

(249) Sky Pilot 12c ★★★★★ ❏

18 bolts to a double ring anchor, **36m/120' – lower with a 70-meter rope.** This route starts eight feet right of *Original Sin* and climbs the low-angled slab to a high first bolt. Climb the face right of the dihedral system, before moving up and left onto a smooth face at mid-height. Above this face, climb the left side of the arête on large features that get progressively smaller, before a difficult sequence back around the arête to the right that leads to the anchors. FA: Louie Anderson 2005.

(250) Violator 11c ★★★★★ ❏

12 bolts to a triple ring anchor, **33m/110' – lower with a 70-meter rope**. You can use a 60-meter rope if you start off and lower to the original starting ledge. This route now has an optional lower start. Start off the ground below *Sky Pilot's* ledge. Climb past two bolts to reach the original starting ledge. Above the ledge, steep moves follow the discontinuous flake system. One of the better and more popular 5.11's in the Quarry. FA: Louie Anderson 2004.

(251) Wicked Violator 5.13b ★★★★ ❏

19 bolts to 2 open shuts, **52m/170' L-P-L** will only work with a 70-meter rope when starting from the lower ground start. If using a 60-meter rope you must belay from the ledge (original) start to ensure that you have enough rope length to safely L-P-L. The extension to *Violator*. When you reach the end of that route continue past the anchor and climb through a big bulge. Quality climbing right to the end. FA: Louie Anderson 2004.

(252) Lothario 13c ★★★★ ❏

20 bolts to a double ring anchor, **42m/140' L-P-L.** An alternate extension to *Violator*. Climb that route and when you reach the belay ledge, clip the anchors on the right extreme of the ledge and continue through the bulge on small crimps, moving up and right. After clipping two bolts, join *Temptation Supreme* at its fifteenth bolt. Finish on that route. FA: Bront Webster 2006.

Taboo Area • Route Profile

Taboo
ROUTE PROFILE

Climber: Joshua Higgins   Photos: Andre Kiryanov

Taboo Area • Route Profile

(248) Taboo 12c ★★★★★

For complete route description see page 141

Easily the best crack route in the Quarry, this beautiful line was first climbed as an aid route. When Louie Anderson first climbed it on aid, he thought it was a good candidate to try and free climb. He succeeded in doing just that in 2003 as one of his first efforts in the new wave of development at the crag.

A short bolted section of steep face leads up and right from the ledge at the end of your choice of approach pitches. Once the dihedral is reached, very solid protection can be had with small cams and the occasional stopper. What starts as a relatively easy lieback crack, quickly turns into a stemming challenge as both walls of the dihedral get much steeper at mid-height.

This amazing route should be on any crack climber's tick list.

Taboo Area • Route Profile

Violator
ROUTE PROFILE

Climber: Ashley Jay

Taboo Area • Route Profile

250 Violator 11c ★★★★★

For complete route description see page 141

One of the most popular 5.11's at the crag, *Violator* offers steep, gymnastic climbing on perfect quality rock. The discontinuous flake system that defines the line of the climbing is for the most part pretty positive. It's the sections between the flakes that provides the challenge; whether it be the midway crux crimps on a smooth and steep panel of rock, or the pumpy moves on the flat, finishing edges, found after the flakes disappear altogether.

Many a climber starts this route feeling strong, only to battle the pump on the insecure moves to the ledge at the top of the climb. Some choose to sprint their way up the route in a race against time, while others milk the rests at the positive flakes. Regardless of your approach, try to ensure that you've got a little gas left in your tank when you reach the top.

This route can also be used to access the top anchors of the crimping test piece, *Seduction*, located just to the right. Those anchors are found on the right end of the same ledge as the anchors of *Violator*.

Taboo Area

㉕㉝ Seduction 12d ★★★★ ☐

12 bolts to a double ring anchor, 30m/100'. This and the following four routes start off a small platform twenty feet up and right from the low start of *Violator*. This platform is located beneath a large, left-facing dihedral. Climb straight up the left side of the face, following a left-facing flake and crack system. After reaching the end of this crack system (just below a small roof), clip the fifth bolt just above the roof and move up and right onto the smooth, overhanging face. A long series of crimps and sequential moves leads to a slight depression mid-way up the route. Climb the steeper bulge above this depression, finishing up the left side of the upper arête. Ends at anchors on the right end of the *Violator* ledge. FA: Louie Anderson 2006

㉕㊃ Seduction Supreme 13c ★★★★ ☐

20 bolts to a double ring anchor, **44m/145' L-P-L (145 feet).** The extension to *Seduction*. Climb that route and after clipping it's anchors, follow the line of *Lothario* to join and finish on *Temptation Supreme*. FA: Louie Anderson 2007.

㉕㊄ Temptation 12d ★★★ ☐

10 bolts to a double ring anchor, 27m/90'. This route begins as for *Seduction,* but after clipping that route's second bolt, move up and right following the bolt line up a technical face to anchors on a ledge system. FA: Louie Anderson 2004.

㉕㊅ Temptation Supreme 13d ★★★★★ ☐

19 bolts to a double ring anchor, **44m/145' L-P-L.** The extension to *Temptation*. Upon reaching the anchors of that route, climb up and right then back left through a bulge. Continue on the thin upper face, before ultimately finishing up positive flakes. The anchors are guarded by a heart-breaker move 125 feet above the start. OB: Louie Anderson 2004. FA: Chris Linder 2006

㉕㊆ Forbidden Fruit 12a ★★★★★ ☐

18 bolts to 2 open shuts, **45m/150' L-P-L.** Start just right of *Temptation* and climb the clean stemming corner. After the dihedral a steep face and seam lead to an exposed, gold-colored corner and the beautiful upper flake. FA: Louie Anderson 2003.

㉕㊇ Magic Mushroom 11b ★★★ ☐

9 bolts to a double chain anchor, 26m/85'. This route begins at ground level, below and just to the right of the *Forbidden Fruit* belay platform. Climb the right side of the arête and climb past two bolts to reach the large ledge. Above this ledge, continue up the right side of the long, low-angled arête. OB: Brent Webster. FA: Gary Henning 2004.

㉕㊈ Handful of Harpies 11c ★★ ☐

8 bolts to a double chain anchor, 26m/85'. Begin climbing twenty feet right of the *Magic Mushroom* arête, at a pair of parallel seams. Large features lead to a high first bolt. Continue climbing past this bolt up the center of the pillar, past two more bolts, to reach a shallow ledge. Climb past this ledge and finish up the center of the face, ending at shared anchors with *Magic Mushroom*. FA: Gary Henning 2006.

Taboo Area

Aaron Cassebeer on Orginal Sin (11b)

ⓨ First Born 13b ★★★ ❑

12 bolts to a double ring anchor, 26m/85'. This route begins at the anchors of *Magic Mushroom*. A difficult mantle is followed by delicate climbing up and right on the upper face. A boulder problem out the bulge at mid-height leads to low-angled, yet still challenging, climbing right before the high anchors. FA: Brian Cullen 2006.

ⓨ Cavorting 10d ★★ ❑

6 bolts to a double chain anchor, 24m/80'. This route begins thirty feet right of *Handful of Harpies*, on the right side of the large boulder. Start at a thin right-facing lieback crack and follow it to the high first bolt. Continue up blocky and shattered terrain. After clipping the fifth bolt, traverse left and then mantle up into a shallow depression, before moving back right to finish the route at anchors on the big ledge. This is the free version of *Run Amok's* original first pitch, which may or may not have been free climbed. FA: Mark Smith, Richard Jenson 1982. Bolts by Gary Henning 2004.

Taboo Area

㉒ Run Amok 11b ★★★ ❏

22 bolts to a double ring anchor, **45m/150' L-P-L.** This line was one of the original routes that saw free climbing efforts. It first contained sections of aid and free climbing, but over the years the aid sections were eliminated one by one. By using large, blocky features, the climbing was not as difficult as you would imagine, given the angle and length of the wall. Unfortunately, the majority of those features have since fallen off or been removed and the route is now substantially different. Begin by climbing *Cavorting,* but after clipping the seventh bolt, move right to clip a high bolt on the right face. Hand traverse the edge of the face above this bolt to gain the obvious horn and continue up and right through the bulge. Fun moves up the right side of a shallow arête lead to a high bulge and the 100' anchors. The route continues past those anchors through a pair of bulges. Continue slightly up and right along a delicate traverse to reach the steep flakes at the finish. Using long draws or slings will keep the rope drag manageable on this wandering line.
FA: Mark Smith, Richard Jensen 1982. FFA (current version): Louie Anderson 2007.

㉓ Purple Haze 12b ★★★ ❏

20 bolts to a double ring anchor, **48m/160' L-P-L.** *With rope stretch, it's OK to L-P-L using a 60-meter rope, but please be careful or use a 70-meter rope.* Begin as for Run Amok, but shortly after the star of the lieback crack, move straight up to the large, obvious features. Continue along the bolt line and climb the steep, rippled face, trending up and right. Follow the right corner system above this face through multiple small bulges to finish at anchors at the top of the wall.
FA: Brent Webster 2003.

㉔ Solidarity 12b ★★★★ ❏

22 bolts to a double ring anchor, **47m/155' L-P-L**. This route begins thirty feet uphill and to the right of *Purple Haze* on top of the talus pile. Start climbing at a finger crack in the remnants of one of the original drill flutes to reach a moderately high first bolt. Continue up and left, following a shallow corner system above a rust-colored section of rock. Climb the tall face, just left of the drill flute, and finish at shared anchors with *Purple Haze.* FA: Louie Anderson 2005.

㉕ Runaway 12a ★★★ ❏

16 bolts to a double chain anchor, **45m/150' L-P-L.** Climbs the blocky face ten feet right of *Solidarity,* just right of the left of two long drill flutes. It begins off the top of the large flake and climbs to a high first bolt. A sustained and pumpy endeavor that's pretty popular. FA: Grahm Doe 2003.

㉖ Momentum 12b ★★★★ ❏

19 bolts to a double ring anchor, **L-P-L (155 feet).** Begin climbing just right of the starting flake of *Runaway* and follow a crack system to the first bolt. Climb up and slightly left through the smooth face. A sequential boulder problem low leads to easier and enjoyable climbing up the center of the tall face. FA: Louie Anderson 2005.

㉗ Rocky 11d ★★★ ❏

17 bolts to a double ring anchor. **L-P-L (150 feet).** One of the first sport routes at the crag. Begin climbing at the right of the two long drill flutes. Clip a high first bolt and continue to the top of the wall climbing along the flanks of the drill flute. Similar to, but slightly easier and less sustained than, *Runaway.* FA: Grahm Doe 2003.

Chris Lindner on Temptation Supreme (13d)

Taboo Area • Route Profile

Forbidden Fruit
ROUTE PROFILE

Climber: Louie Anderson *Photos: Perri Nguyen*

Taboo Area • Route Profile

257 Forbidden Fruit 12a
★★★★★

For complete route description see page 146

Perhaps there is no 5.12 in the Quarry more diverse than *Forbidden Fruit*. The route begins with technical face climbing and stemming up an obvious corner. This is followed by a short bulge and a balancey seam. After clipping the 100-foot anchors, a steeper stemming corner leads to the long upper flake system. 145 feet into the route, the climber is then faced with an insecure sequence just before the anchors. There are two ways to do this sequence, equally difficult, and many climbers fail spitting distance from the end.

On the first ascent, the upper flake was led on thin gear. Because so much of the remainder of the route was bolted, the decision was made to bolt this section of climbing as well. However, the bolts are a little spaced and you may want to carry some small stoppers or micro-cams to supplement the bolts.

While reviewing the responses from locals when asked which routes were worthy of profiling, this route was on almost everyone's list. Many people called it the best 5.12 at the crag; and a handful called it the best route at the crag. That's pretty high praise, but it's well-deserved. Climb it and see for yourself...

The Alcove

152 • Climber's Guide: Riverside Quarry

The Alcove

- (268) Shwazzle Dazzle 11c ★★★★
- (269) Crazy Town 13b ★★★
- (270) Procrastination 12c ★★★
- (271) Ghetto Fabulous 12d ★★★★
- (272) Toothless Tweaker 12c ★★★
- (273) Tweaker 13b ★★★★
- (274) Character Assassination 12a ★★★
- (275) Love 12b ★★★
- (276) Love and Theft 13a ★★★★
- (277) Hand Me Down 12a ★★★
- (278) Hands of Time 13a ★★★★
- (279) Short Shot 11a ★★★
- (280) Long Shot 12b ★★★
- (281) Pith 12b ★★★
- (282) Pith Monster 13a ★★★
- (283) Fractional 12a ★★★
- (284) Fractional Envy 12d ★★★
- (285) Infinite 13c ★★★
- (286) Infinite Jest – project ★★★
- (287) Debut 12c ★★
- (288) Debutaunt 13c ★★★
- (289) Yellow Fever 10d ★★
- (290) Hysteria 12d ★★★
- (291) Doctor Greenthumb 10b ★
- (292) Cornered 11d ★
- (293) Seamstress 13a ★★

The Alcove is found directly right of the Taboo Area, and is home to the highest concentration of long (over 100-foot) pitches at the crag. The standout routes in this area are: *Short Shot* (11a), *Shwazzle Dazzle* (11c), *Ghetto Fabulous* (12d), *Love and Theft* (13a), and *Hands of Time* (13a).

Routes are described from left to right.

(268) Shwazzle Dazzle 11c ★★★★ ☐

12 bolts to 2 open shuts, 30m/100'. This route is found at the far left of the area, and begins just before the base drops off to the lower level. Climb up a series of right-facing flakes and corners, before turning a roof just after the fifth bolt. Continue up the right-facing features above, leading to the crux traverse up and right, just before the anchors. FA: Brent Webster 2005.

(269) Crazy Town 13b ★★★ ☐

20 bolts to a double ring anchor, **42m/140' L-P-L.** The extension to *Shwazzle Dazzle*. After clipping that route's anchors, continue straight up and over the obvious bulge above. Slopey arête moves over the bulge require cooler conditions for success. FA: Brent Webster 2005.

The Alcove

❷⓻⓪ Procrastination 12c
★★★ ☐

15 bolts to a double ring anchor, 35m/115' - 70-meter rope to lower. This route begins six feet right of *Shwazzle Dazzle,* and climbs up the center of the face, passing many small bulges. FA: Louie Anderson 2008.

❷⓻❶ Ghetto Fabulous 12d
★★★★ ☐

22 bolts to a double ring anchor, 44m/145' L-P-L. Starts at the right-facing dihedral, twelve feet right of *Procrastination.* Follow the crack in the dihedral and after clipping the third bolt, continue up and right, following a blocky corner system. Continue up right-facing features and after clipping the 100-foot anchors, continue up the very steep summit bulge. FA: Louie Anderson 2005.

❷⓻❷ Toothless Tweaker 12c
★★★ ☐

11 bolts to a double ring anchor, 30m/100'. This route begins twelve feet right of *Ghetto Fabulous,* and climbs up to and over a low bulge. Continue up dished terrain, left of the drill flute, to anchors at the 100-foot level. FA: Louie Anderson 2007.

❷⓻❸ Tweaker 13b
★★★★ ☐

19 bolts to a double ring anchor, **42m/140' L-P-L.** The extension to *Toothless Tweaker.* After clipping that route's anchors, continue up to and through the steep bulge above on crimps, before moving up and left to finish at the anchors of *Ghetto Fabulous.* FA: Louie Anderson 2007.

Louie Anderson sticking the crux on Fusion (14b)
Photo: Matt Callender

The Alcove

❷⓻❹ Character Assassination 12a ★★★ ☐

22 bolts to double chain anchor, **42m/140' L-P-L.** This route begins twelve feet right of *Toothless Tweaker*, just right of a shallow corner system. Climb up to a shallow, sloped ledge and continue up the face above, climbing on the right side of the drill flute. A long and enjoyable route. FA: Gary Henning 2009.

❷⓻❺ Love 12b ★★★ ☐

10 bolts to a double chain anchor, 30m/100'. Climb the left-facing flake eight feet right of *Character Assassination*. Continue up the center of the low face. After a rest at the depressed ledge, continue through many bulges up the center of the face. Traverse right at the end of the route to reach anchors on the ledge. FA: Gary Henning 2008.

❷⓻❻ Love and Theft 13a ★★★★ ☐

17 bolts to a double ring anchor, **41m/135' L-P-L.** Climb *Love*, but instead of traversing to clip its anchors, continue up the shallow, right-facing dihedral and the face above, leading to the high, obvious roof. Sequential moves through this roof lead to the anchors. FA: Gary Henning 2008.

❷⓻❼ Hand Me Down 12a ★★★ ☐

12 bolts to double chain anchor, 29m/95'. This route starts four feet right of *Love and Theft* and climbs up the center of the low block, to the ledge above the first bolt. A delicate sequence on the short face above this ledge leads to another bulge. Following this bulge, a long and enjoyable face leads to the anchors. FA: Gary Henning 2006.

❷⓻❽ Hands of Time 13a ★★★★ ☐

19 bolts to a double chain anchor, **42m/140' L-P-L.** The extension to *Hands of Time*. After clipping that route's anchors, continue up the steep face above to anchors at the top of the cliff. FA: Gary Henning 2006.

❷⓻❾ Short Shot 11a ★★★ ☐

9 bolts to a double ring anchor, 29m/95'. This route starts twenty feet up and right from *Hands of Time*, on an upper level. Climb up to and over many blocky bulges to anchors on a ledge at the 95-foot level. Good warm-up for the harder routes in the area. FA: Gary Henning 2006.

❷❽⓿ Long Shot 12b ★★★ ☐

16 bolts to a double ring anchor, **42m/140' L-P-L.** The extension to *Short Shot*. After clipping that route's anchors, continue to the top of the wall. FA: Gary Henning 2006

❷❽❶ Pith 12b ★★★ ☐

11 bolts to a double ring anchor, 30m/100' This route starts eight feet right of *Short Shot* and climbs a short, smooth lower face to a big ledge. Continue above this ledge, before climbing slightly up and left to anchors at 100 feet. FA: Gary Henning 2006.

❷❽❷ Pith Monotor 13a ★★★ ☐

19 bolts to a double ring anchor, **41m/135' L-P-L.** The extension to *Pith*. After clipping that route's anchors, continue to the top of the wall, passing a difficult crux sequence. FA: Gary Henning 2007.

The Alcove

ⓧ Fractional 12a ★★★ ☐

6 bolts to a double chain anchor, 18m/60'. This route starts twenty feet up and right from *Pith Monster*, on an upper ledge. Metal rungs lead to this ledge. Begin climbing off the top of the ground level boulder and climb easy features to the high first bolt. Continue through blocky and bulging terrain up the long face. FA: Gary Henning 2006.

ⓧ Fractional Envy 12d ★★★ ☐

15 bolts to a double ring anchor, **41m/120' L-P-L or lower with a 70-meter rope.** The extension to *Fractional*. Climb that route and then continue through the high bulge and finish on the smooth upper face. FA: Gary Henning 2006.

ⓧ Infinite 13c ★★★ ☐

8 bolts to a ring anchor, 21m/70'. This route begins six feet right of *Fractional Envy*. Climb up onto a large ledge system. A difficult boulder problem off this ledge leads up and right to the obvious left-facing dihedral. The route climbs the right side of the arête forming this dihedral and finishes up a smooth slab in the middle of the cliff to anchors at the 70-foot level. FA: Gary Henning 2009.

ⓧ Infinite Jest – project ★★★ ☐

15 bolts to a double chain anchor, **42m/120' L-P-L or lower with a 70-meter rope.** The extension to *Infinite*. After clipping the anchors, move up and right to reach another dihedral system leading to a hard bulge and the summit headwall. FA: Gary Henning 2011.

ⓧ Debut 12c ★★ ☐

6 bolts to a double ring anchor, 14m/45'. This route starts twelve feet right of *Infinite Jest*. After climbing up onto the ledge system, continue up the smooth face and through a short, bulging headwall. Difficult moves leading left through this headwall lead to enjoyable slab climbing and anchors at 45 feet. FA: Gary Henning 2007.

ⓧ Debutaunt 13c ★★★ ☐

13 bolts to a double chain anchor, **41m/120' L-P-L or lower with a 70-meter rope.** The extension to *Debut*. Instead of clipping that route's anchors, continue up the face before moving right and over a large bulge. A deadpoint crux at the top of this bulge leads to easier climbing up a second bulge, before finishing up the dihedral above. FA: Gary Henning 2009.

ⓧ Yellow Fever 10d ★★ ☐

6 bolts to a double ring anchor, 14m/45'. This route begins ten feet right of *Debutaunt* and climbs over ledgey terrain to reach the obvious left-facing dihedral. Climb the face just left of the dihedral. FA: Brent Webster 2006.

ⓧ Hysteria 12d ★★★ ☐

15 bolts to a double ring anchor, **35m/115' - 70-meter rope to lower.** This route is located above *Yellow Fever*. After clipping that route's anchors, continue up and right and climb over the short, steep face to reach a left-facing flake system. At the top of these flakes, continue up the arête above to finish on the smooth slab. FA: Brent Webster 2009.

The Alcove

291 Doctor Greenthumb 10b ★ ❏

6 bolts to a double ring anchor, 14m/45'. This route climbs up and right onto the large granite block to the right of *Yellow Fever's* start. Move around the right side of the quartz arête and continue up the right side of this feature. After clipping the third bolt, and reaching the top of the pillar, climb up to a large block and finish up the left side of this block to anchors in a shallow dihedral feature. FA: Josh Ogle 2006.

292 Cornered 11d ★ ❏

8 bolts to a double ring anchor, 14m/45'. This route is found twenty feet to the right of the start of *Doctor Greenthumb* and begins on the right side of a sharp arête. Climb the arête and continue up blocky terrain to reach a short, left-facing dihedral. Stemming up this corner leads to the route's anchors. FA: Gary Henning 2006.

293 Seamstress 13a ★★ ❏

14 bolts to a double ring anchor, **35m/115' - 70-meter rope to lower.** The extension to *Cornered*. After clipping the ledge anchors of that route, continue up to and over the bulge above. A smooth headwall ultimately leads to a left-trending dihedral flake and the route's anchors. FA: Brent Webster 2008.

Matt Callender on Procrastination (11d)

Schoolhouse Rock

Schoolhouse Rock

- ㉔ Schoolhouse Rock 5.8 ★
- ㉕ The Check's in the Mail 5.7 ★★
- ㉖ The Energy Blues 5.6 ★★
- ㉗ Taxman Max 5.5 ★
- ㉘ Dollars and Sense 5.7 ★
- ㉙ Tyrannosaurus Debt 5.9 ★
- ㉚ I'm Just a Bill 5.6 ★
- ㉛ My Hero Zero 5.0
- ㉜ Conjunction Junction 5.9 ★★
- ㉝ Function Junction 5.9 ★
- ㉞ What's Your Function? 10b ★★
- ㉟ Interplanet Janet 5.6 ★★★
- ㊱ House of Cards 10b ★
- ㊲ Victim of Gravity 10a ★★

Schoolhouse Rock is located to the right and downhill from The Alcove. The area was developed in the hope of creating a resource for beginning leaders and for climbers who would like to bring out less-experienced friends or groups. The routes found here are much shorter and less steep than other Quarry offerings, and by extension less intimidating. Many of the routes share anchors with their neighbors and this makes setting up topropes much easier and more efficient. The better routes include *Interplanet Janet* (5.6), *The Energy Blues* (5.6), *The Check's in the Mail* (5.7), and *Conjunction Junction* (5.9).

Schoolhouse Rock

Routes are described from left to right.

㉚ Schoolhouse Rock 5.8 ★ ❏

5 bolts to a double chain anchor, 11m/35'. This route begins at the left end of the formation and climbs the center of a smooth, low-angle slab to the first bolt. Climb over a series of three overlaps to reach the anchors on an upper slab. FA: Craig Britton, Chris Miller 2008.

㉛ The Check's in the Mail 5.7 ★★ ❏

7 bolts to a double ring anchor, 14m/45'. Begin climbing ten feet right of *Schoolhouse Rock*. Climb the low-angle slab to a bolt in the steeper face. Pass this face and continue on the slab above. After clipping the third bolt, move up and right to join *Energy Blues* at that route's fourth bolt. Finish on that route. FA: Chris Miller 2008.

㉜ The Energy Blues 5.6 ★★ ❏

8 bolts to a double ring anchor, 14m/45'. This route climbs the recessed face eight feet right of *The Check's in the Mail*. After clipping the fourth bolt, continue up the smooth center of the face. Finish up a short steep section to reach the anchors. FA: Louie Anderson 2008.

㉝ Taxman Max 5.5 ★ ❏

6 bolts to a double chain anchor, 12m/40'. Start as for *The Energy Blues*, but after clipping the second bolt, move up and right into the left-facing dihedral. A mantle at the top of the corner leads to shared anchors with *Dollars and Sense*. FA: Louie Anderson 2008.

㉞ Dollars and Sense 5.7 ★ ❏

5 bolts to a double chain anchor, 11m/35'. This route begins eight feet right of *Energy Blues* and climbs the face just right of the arête. A cruxy bulge at mid-height provides the difficulty on the route. FA: Euan Cameron, Chris Miller 2007.

㉟ Tyrannosaurus Debt 5.9 ★ ❏

6 bolts to a double chain anchor, 12m/40'. Start climbing just right of *Dollars and Sense*. Slab moves lead past four bolts, before moving left to join *Dollars and Sense* at its fourth bolt. Finish on that route. FA: Chris Miller, Isaac Tait 2007.

㉠ I'm Just a Bill 5.6 ★ ❏

7 bolts to a double ring anchor, 12m/40'. This route starts fifteen feet right of *Tyrannosaurus Debt* and climbs the low-angled slab past a bolt to reach a short, vertical crack. Continue up the face above to reach anchors at the high ledge. FA: Louie Anderson 2008.

㉡ My Hero Zero 5.0

7 bolts to a double ring anchor, 12m/40'. Climb the low-angled and heavily-featured face fifteen feet up and right of *I'm Just a Bill*. Finish at shared anchors with that route. FA: Louie Anderson 2008.

㉢ Conjunction Junction 5.9 ★★ ❏

9 bolts to a double ring anchor, 17m/55'. Starting eight feet right of *My Hero Zero*, climb up and right over a short corner feature. Continue straight up the steepening slab to reach a short headwall before the anchors. FA: Louie Anderson 2008.

Schoolhouse Rock

Kayla Anderson on I'm Just a Bill (5.6)

Schoolhouse Rock

303 Function Junction 5.9 ★

8 bolts to a double ring anchor, 14m/45'. A link up. Begin as for *What's Your Function,* but after clipping that route's fifth bolt, move left, passing one independent bolt, to join *Conjunction Junction* at its eighth bolt. Finish on that route. FA: Louie Anderson 2008.

304 What's Your Function? 10b ★★

6 bolts to a double ring anchor, 12m/40'. This route starts fifteen feet uphill and right from *Conjunction Junction.* Climb the obvious left-facing corner system. After clipping the fifth bolt, continue straight up, over the bulge above. FA: Louie Anderson 2008.

305 Interplanet Janet 5.6 ★★★

5 bolts to a double ring anchor, 11m/35'. Start climbing at the right edge of the face, six feet right of *What's Your Function.* Follow the blocky corner system to reach the ledge below a short bulge. Traverse left and then follow the positive flake up and right to reach the anchors. FA: Louie Anderson 2008.

306 House of Cards 10b ★

7 bolts to a double ring anchor, 15m/50'. This route begins ten feet uphill and to the right of *Interplanet Janet.* Climb up to the first of several overlaps and continue straight up the face to anchors at the top of the formation. FA: Louie Anderson 2008.

307 Victim of Gravity 10a ★★

7 bolts to a double ring anchor, 14m/45'. Climb the overlap onto the slab just left of the right edge of the formation, about twenty-five feet uphill from *House of Cards.* Continue up and left through a series of shallow overlaps, before finishing up the crack system above. Shares the last bolt with *House of Cards* and finishes on that route. FA: Louie Anderson 2008.

Julian Bautista on Delirious (11b)

Fun Factory

The Fun Factory

- ⬤ Fun Factory 5.7 ★★★★
- ⬤ Planned Obsolescence 5.9 ★★
- ⬤ Made to Order 10a ★★★
- ⬤ Structural Flaw 10b ★★★★
- ⬤ Mass Production 10b ★★★
- ⬤ Industrial Bliss 10a ★★★★
- ⬤ Worker Bee 10b ★★★★
- ⬤ Manufacturer's Defect 10c ★★★
- ⬤ Assembly Line 10d ★★★
- ⬤ Quality Control 10c ★★★
- ⬤ Nuts and Bolts 10c ★★
- ⬤ Six Sigma Certified 10b ★
- ⬤ Some Assembly Required 10c ★★
- ⬤ Union Man 11a ★

The Fun Factory is located around the right side of the hill from Schoolhouse Rock. It sits at the top of a short slope, just left of the Agony Arch Area. Due to the techniques used to develop this wall, a little longer introduction text is probably in order.

The Quarry is a wonderful sport climbing resource, however it has always been lacking in routes within the 5.10 rating. Those who climb at this level continue to repeat the same routes over and over, simply because there are no other options at the cliff. As a result, these routes are often very crowded on popular days.

Fun Factory

When working on this edition of the guidebook, Louie Anderson once again took a look at this wall. It was often dismissed as being too blank and chossy to bolt, which it was. The surface layer of rock on the majority of the wall was scaly, decomposed granite that was not conducive to climbing at all. He saw the cliff as more or less of a blank canvas, and enlisted Gary Henning to help create routes on the wall.

This cliff has by far the highest concentration of manufactured holds at the crag. 5.11, 5.12 and 5.13 routes could have been created on the wall with far less manufacturing, but the crag already has several routes at those levels, and from the beginning the goal was to try and fill a void with whatever routes were the end result of the work. That work is now complete. The wall offers fourteen new, moderate routes; all but one of which are 5.10 and easier. The wall is steeper than many of the other moderate offerings at the crag and compliments the many slabs found here and there within the Quarry at these difficulty levels. The cliff is also shorter than most of the other cliffs. Because of this, its routes are less intimidating and require less endurance to succeed on. The routes are quite fun and will hopefully be well-received. The standout lines are *Fun Factory* (5.7), *Industrial Bliss* (10a), *Structural Flaw* (10b), *Worker Bee* (10b), and *Quality Control* (10c).

The wall enjoys mixed shade in the morning, with the leftmost routes going into the sun first. Routes are described from left to right.

308 Fun Factory 5.7 ★★★★ ❏

7 bolts to a double ring anchor, 14m/45'. This climb is found at the far left end of the face, and begins at a smooth brown slab. Climb the blocky corner system, joining *Planned Obsolescence* after the fifth bolt. FA: Louie Anderson 2011.

309 Planned Obsolescence 5.9 ★★ ❏

6 bolts to a double ring anchor, 12m/40'. Climbs the shallow, brown buttress twenty feet right of *Fun Factory*. Ends at shared anchors with *Fun Factory*. FA: Gary Henning 2011.

310 Made to Order 10a ★★★ ❏

6 bolts to a double ring anchor, 12m/40'. Begin climbing off the top of a long, low rock at the point where the rock turns from brown to gray. After clipping the first bolt, move through a series of underclings and continue on positive features to the top of the wall. FA: Louie Anderson 2011.

311 Structural Flaw 10b ★★★★ ❏

7 bolts to a double ring anchor, 17m/55'. A link up. Begin as for *Mass Production*, but after clipping the fourth bolt, move up and left following the flake past two independent bolts to join *Made to Order* at its last bolt. Finish on that route. FA: Louie Anderson 2011.

312 Mass Production 10b ★★★ ❏

6 bolts to a double ring anchor, 14m/45'. This route begins fifteen feet right of *Made to Order* and climbs the faint water streak. After clipping the fourth bolt, continue straight up. FA: Louie Anderson 2011.

Fun Factory

Ashley Jay on Industrial Bliss (10a)

⬤313 Industrial Bliss 10a ★★★★ ❑

8 bolts to a double ring anchor, 17m/55'. This route starts eight feet right of *Mass Production*, off the top of a small rock. Climb straight up on positive features, to the obvious diagonal crack and the left edge of a shallow roof. Pass this roof on its left side and continue to the top of the wall on positive pockets. A popular line that is one of the best 5.10's at the crag. FA: Louie Anderson 2011.

Fun Factory

🔵314 Worker Bee 10b ★★★★ ❏

9 bolts to a double ring anchor, 18m/60'. Begin climbing eight feet right and downhill from *Industrial Bliss*, off the long, lower platform. Climb straight up to and over the shallow roof at mid-height, on positive features. Finish up the headwall above. The longest route on the wall. FA: Louie Anderson 2011.

🔵315 Manufacturer's Defect 10c ★★★ ❏

8 bolts to a double ring anchor, 17m/55' This route begins eight feet right of *Worker Bee*. Climb the face just right of the roof. FA: Louie Anderson 2011.

🔵316 Assembly Line 10d ★★★ ❏

7 bolts to a double ring anchor, 15m/50'. Found twenty-five feet right and uphill from *Manufacturer's Defect*, this route follow the left-diagonalling feature. After clipping the first bolt, continue up and left on positive holds and follow the bolt line that crosses the left edge of a short overlap. FA: Louie Anderson 2011.

🔵317 Quality Control 10c ★★★ ❏

7 bolts to a double ring anchor, 14m/45'. Begin as for *Assembly Line*, but after clipping that route's first bolt, climb straight up the center of the smooth face. Cross the overlap at its right edge and finish up positive flakes. FA: Louie Anderson 2011.

🔵318 Nuts and Bolts 10c ★★ ❏

5 bolts to a double ring anchor, 11m/35'. This route is located twelve feet up and right from *Quality Control*. Preclip the first bolt, before stepping left off the block. Climb the short face on small, but positive features. FA: Gary Henning 2011.

🔵319 Six Sigma Certified 10b ★ ❏

4 bolts to a double ring anchor, 11m/35'. Begin a few feet right of *Nuts and Bolts*, and climb the right side of the face on large features. Some longer reaches on this one, require shorter climbers to step high. FA: Jim Parisi 2011.

🔵320 Some Assembly Required 10c ★★ ❏

7 bolts to a double ring anchor, 14m/45'. Climbs the corner system eight feet right of *Six Sigma Certified*. Easy terrain leads to a traverse left through the bulge, following a positive flake. After turning the lip, finish on the left, upper face using positive flakes and edges. FA: Louie Anderson 2011.

🔵321 Union Man 11a ★ ❏

6 bolts to a double ring anchor, 11m/35'. Begin climbing ten feet right and downhill from *Some Assembly Required*. Easier climbing up the lower ramp leads to a long move to a pocket in the roof. Campus moves around the lip of the roof lead to an easier finish. FA: Gary Henning 2011.

Fun Factory
ROUTE PROFILE

Climber: Mike Heredia

Fun Factory • Route Profile

308 Fun Factory 5.7 ★★★★

For complete route description see page 163

With the development of The Fun Factory, the Quarry now has a good concentration of more moderate routes. This particular route is the easiest on the wall and one of the most popular. The steep corner and ramp system is filled with positive holds and interesting movement, making this climb the best offering under 5.10 at the crag. It's a good introduction to the steeper climbing found elsewhere on this and other Quarry walls.

Beginning on a smooth section of slab, this great route tests climbers' footwork before rewarding them with more positive holds through the steep, middle section of the route. A high traverse right on flat edges, once again rewards the climber with positive holds through a final bulge. Easier climbing then leads to anchors on the protruding summit visor.

Fun Factory shares anchors with the slightly harder route to the right and climbing it is a good way to set up a top rope on that fun line. Due to the diagonal nature of the climbing, it's easiest to toprope the route to clean it.

Agony Arch Area

Agony Arch Area

- ③²² **Stemsation 10a** ★★★
- ③²³ **Chupacabra 11a** ★★★
- ③²⁴ **The Degenerate 12b** ★
- ³²⁵ **Delinquency 11a** ★★★
- ³²⁶ **Corruption 12c** ★★
- ³²⁷ **Debauchery 12d** ★★
- ³²⁸ **Stem Job 11a** ★
- ³²⁹ **Every Dog Has His Day**
- ³³⁰ **Sweet Agony 13b** ★★★
- ³³¹ **Agony Arch 11b** ★★★★★
- ³³² **Escape from Agony 11b** ★★★
- ³³³ **Hump or Dump 10a** ★★
- ³³⁴ **Pimp Chimp 12c** ★★
- ³³⁵ **Ramp Champ 11a** ★★
- ³³⁶ **Quake and Shake Flakes 10d** ★★
- ³³⁷ **Valiant Flail to No Avail 11c** ★★
- ³³⁸ **Fear the Smear 5.8** ★

This area is found just right of The Fun Factory, and was one of the first sections of the cliff to see free climbing interest. It is home to Chris Robbins' historic climb *Agony Arch* (11b), one of the first 5.11's in southern California. Most of the routes here are quite short by Quarry standards and offer a welcome change from the longer routes found around on the main walls. The best routes in the area include: *Stemsation* (10a), *Delinquency* (11a), *Agony Arch* (11b) and *Sweet Agony* (13b).

Agony Arch Area

Routes are described left to right.

③²² Stemsation 10a ★★★ ☐
4 bolts to a double ring anchor, 9m/30'. This route is found at the far left edge of the face and climbs the obvious right-facing corner. A series of side pulls at the top of the route lead through steep terrain to anchors at the top of the face. FA: Louie Anderson 2011.

³²³ Chupacabra 11a ★★★ ☐
5 bolts to 2 open shuts, 9m/30'. This climb starts eight feet of *Stemsation*, at the right end of the platform. Climb the steepening face on edges and crimps. FA: Louie Anderson 2003.

³²⁴ The Degenerate 12b ★ ☐
5 bolts to 2 open shuts, 11m/35'. This route is found twelve feet right and downhill from *Chupacabra*. Climb the face up to and over a bulge, before moving right to the anchors. FA: Louie Anderson 2003.

³²⁵ Delinquency 11a ★★★ ☐
5 bolts to 2 open shuts, 12m/40'. This classic route climbs the right arête and the face above on sometimes balancey moves. Shares anchors with *The Degenerate*. FA: Louie Anderson 2003.

³²⁶ Corruption 12c ★★ ☐
5 bolts to 2 open shuts, 12m/40'. Considerably more challenging than it appears, this route follows the blocky, arched feature ten feet right of the arête as it climbs up and then right. FA: Louie Anderson 2004.

³²⁷ Debauchery 12d ★★ ☐
7 bolts to 2 open shuts, 14m/45'. This route begins twenty feet uphill, to the right of *Corruption*, and about five feet left of the short dihedral. This was once a training route (from the early 90's) made up of glued-on rocks and drilled features. Most of the rocks have fallen off over the years and the current version climbs what remains of the original route. FA: Louie Anderson 2007.

³²⁸ Stem Job 11a ★ ☐
4 bolts to double bolt anchor on ledge, 8m/25'. Climb the thin crack in the short dihedral, just right of *Debauchery*. A miniature route that's actually pretty fun. FA: Unknown.

³²⁹ Every Dog Has His Day
5.9 (tr) 8m/25'. The hangers were removed from this route shortly after it was bolted. Climbs the face six feet right of *Stem Job*. FA: Aaron Rough '95.

³³⁰ Sweet Agony 13b ★★★ ☐
4 bolts and cams to 3"to a double chain anchor, 15m/50'. Start as for *Agony Arch*, but after the first twenty feet move left and follow a diagonal rail system past four bolts. When the rail ends, thin crimping takes you straight up to rejoin and finish on *Agony Arch*. FA: Louie Anderson 2004.

Agony Arch Area

Agony Arch Area

(331) Agony Arch 11b ★★★★★ ☐

Nuts and cams to 4" to a double chain anchor, 15m/50'. The original classic Quarry crack. This route starts forty feet around and to the right from *Every Dog Has His Day*. Climb the shattered crack and flake system to reach the obvious arching crack. As the crack turns more horizontal, continue with either a slopey traverse or fist and off-fist jamming. Once the crack ends a short section of face climbing leads right to anchors on a small ledge. FA: generally attributed to Chris Robbins, et. al. 1977.

(332) Escape from Agony 11b ★★★ ☐

1 bolt, nuts and cams to 2 ½" to a bolt anchor, 15m/50'. Start as for *Agony Arch*, but where it passes a small ledge on the arête to the right climb straight up, away from the crack, passing a bolt as you climb to the top of the formation. FA: Unknown.

(333) Hump or Dump 10a ★★ ☐

2 bolts, nuts and cams to 2" to a double chain anchor, 15m/50'. This route begins ten feet right of *Agony Arch*, and climbs the left-facing thin crack on the corner. Following this crack, climb past two bolts to access the clean diagonal crack. Follow this up and left before following another crack to the right and the anchors. FA: Unknown.

(334) Pimp Chimp 12c ★★ ☐

6 bolts to double chain anchor, 14m/45'. This route is found twenty feet to the right and uphill from *Hump or Dump*. Climb straight up the smooth face, just left of a featured section. Powerful climbing on small holds. Finishes on the upper slab. Be cautious of the difficult second clip. FA: Louie Anderson 2003.

(335) Ramp Champ 11a ★★ ☐

7 bolts to a double chain anchor, 14m/45'. Begin climbing eight feet right of *Pimp Chimp*, and climb straight up the featured face. After clipping that route's fourth bolt traverse left following the obvious ramp, to finish at shared anchors with *Hump or Dump*. FA: Louie Anderson 2003.

(336) Quake and Shake Flakes 10d ★★ ☐

6 bolts to double chain anchor, 14m/45'. Start as for *Ramp Champ*, but after clipping the fourth bolt, continue up and finish on the slab above. FA: Mark Smith, Richard Jensen 1982.

(337) Valiant Flail to No Avail 11c ★★ ☐

5 bolts to double chain anchor, 12m/40'. One of the original Quarry test pieces, this route begins eight feet uphill and to the right of *Quake and Shake Flakes*. Climb to a moderately high first bolt and continue past reachy and hard friction moves to an easier finish. Originally led with only one bolt. FA: Mark Smith 1982.

(338) Fear the Smear 5.8 ★ ☐

5 bolts to double chain anchor, 11m/35'. A short and easy introduction to slab climbing that begins eight feet uphill and to the right of *Valiant Flail to No Avail*. Follow the right line of bolts up the slab. FA: Unknown.

Quarry Grade Dozens

One of the greatest attributes of the climbing at The Quarry is its diversity. Seldom will you find a sport climbing area that has so many different types of climbing, features and movement within a given grade. While a complete listing of routes can be found in the pages immediately following this, below are listed a selected dozen routes in each of the four predominant number grades found at the crag. The quality of these routes contributed to their inclusion on the lists, but the more important factor was the type of climbing found on the route. Collectively, the routes shown on each list offer a wide range of climbing styles, and each list was compiled to highlight the diversity available within that grade.

5.10

American Dream, pitch two   10a   ★★

Stemsation   10a   ★★★

Industrial Bliss   10a   ★★★★

Pleasure Dome   10b   ★★

Flexercise   10b   ★★★★★

Shattered Dreams   10c   ★★

Quality Control   10c   ★★★

Utopia   10c   ★★★

Lovely Lady   10c   ★★★★

Trundle Trophy   10c   ★★★★★

Shockwave   10d   ★★★

Tangerine Dream   10d★★★★★

5.11

Ground Zero   11a   ★★★

Metro   11a   ★★★★

American Dream, pitch three   11b   ★★★★

Vascular Massacre   11b   ★★★★★

Agony Arch   11b   ★★★★★

Flesh and Blood   11b   ★★★★★

Shwazzle Dazzle   11c   ★★★★

Nostalgia   11c   ★★★★★

Violator   11c   ★★★★★

Maximizer   11d   ★★★★

Pursuit of Pain   11d   ★★★★

Leviathan   11d   ★★★★★

Quarry Grade Dozens

Valarie Heredia on Structural Flaw (10b)

5.12

Block Party 12a ★★★

Lucky 12a ★★★★

Forbidden Fruit 12a ★★★★★

Raging Raptor 12a ★★★★★

Gravitational Attraction 12b ★★★

Anger Management 12b ★★★★

Exposure 12b ★★★★

Hanging by a Thread 12b ★★★★★

Sky Pilot 12c ★★★★★

Taboo 12c ★★★★★

Seduction 12d ★★★★

La Bella Donna 12d ★★★★★

5.13

Burly Boogie 13a ★★★

Control Freak 13a ★★★

Hands of Time 13a ★★★★

Vertigo 13a ★★★★

Weapons of Mass Destruction (W.M.D.) 13a ★★★★

King Pin 13a ★★★★★

Gumption 13b ★★★

Tweaker 13b ★★★★

Enigma 13b ★★★★★

Gypsy 13c ★★★★★

Weight of the World 13c ★★★★★

Temptation Supreme 13d ★★★★★

Quarry Routes By Quality

No Star	Page	OS	F	RP
5.0 My Hero Zero	159	❏	❏	❏
5.7 Approach Pitch	61	❏	❏	❏
5.8 One For the Road	66	❏	❏	❏
5.9 Every Dog Has His Day	169	❏	❏	❏

1 Star ★	Page	OS	F	RP
5.5 Taxman Max	159	❏	❏	❏
5.6 I'm Just a Bill	159	❏	❏	❏
5.7 Dollars and Sense	159	❏	❏	❏
5.8 Fear the Smear	171	❏	❏	❏
5.8 Flake and Bake	114	❏	❏	❏
5.8 Hercules Hand Crack	78	❏	❏	❏
5.8 Schoolhouse Rock	159	❏	❏	❏
5.9 Function Junction	161	❏	❏	❏
5.9 Tyrannosaurs Debt	159	❏	❏	❏
10a Scrawny, not Brawny	65	❏	❏	❏
10b Doctor Greenthumb	157	❏	❏	❏
10b House of Cards	161	❏	❏	❏
10b Lowrider	119	❏	❏	❏
10b Six Sigma Certified	165	❏	❏	❏
10c Disco Inferno	114	❏	❏	❏
10c Feetal Rearrangement, pitch two	58	❏	❏	❏
10c Pigeon the Other White Meat	55	❏	❏	❏
10d Cruiser	122	❏	❏	❏
11a Diagonal Direct	55	❏	❏	❏
11a Stem Job	169	❏	❏	❏
11a Union Man	165	❏	❏	❏
11b Bottom Feeder	58	❏	❏	❏
11b Grandma Seizure	61	❏	❏	❏
11b Marathon Man	57	❏	❏	❏
11b Unexpected Difficulties, pitch two	56	❏	❏	❏

Routes by Quality

1 Star ★

	Page	OS	F	RP
11c Burnout	114	❏	❏	❏
11c Chas' Route	58	❏	❏	❏
11c Fiasco	115	❏	❏	❏
11d Cornered	157	❏	❏	❏
11d Mudslinger	112	❏	❏	❏
12b Baby Brigade	66	❏	❏	❏
12b The Degenerate	169	❏	❏	❏
12b Juggernaut	66	❏	❏	❏
12b Spitfire	139	❏	❏	❏
12c Sika Soldier	115	❏	❏	❏

2 Star ★ ★

	Page	OS	F	RP
5.6 The Energy Blues	159	❏	❏	❏
5.7 The Check's in the Mail	159	❏	❏	❏
5.7 Tiptoe	122	❏	❏	❏
5.7 White Light	67	❏	❏	❏
5.8 Feetal Rearrangement, pitch one	58	❏	❏	❏
5.9 Conjunction Junction	159	❏	❏	❏
5.9 Groove Factor	66	❏	❏	❏
5.9 Leapfrog	119	❏	❏	❏
5.9 Planned Obsolescence	163	❏	❏	❏
10a American Dream, pitch two	93	❏	❏	❏
10a Excuse Abuse	70	❏	❏	❏
10a Hump or Dump	171	❏	❏	❏
10a Mantle Marathon	57	❏	❏	❏
10a Minimizer	105	❏	❏	❏
10a Mud Ramp	122	❏	❏	❏
10a Tailspin	119	❏	❏	❏
10a Victim of Gravity	161	❏	❏	❏
10a Victim of Reality	114	❏	❏	❏
10a Whammy	105	❏	❏	❏
10b Baby Face	111	❏	❏	❏
10b Goody Two Shoes	58	❏	❏	❏
10b Jaunt	115	❏	❏	❏
10b Lowrider Direct	121	❏	❏	❏
10b Pleasure Dome	67	❏	❏	❏

Routes by Quality

2 Star ★ ★

Route	Page	OS	F	RP
10b Power Play	105	❏	❏	❏
10b Prisoner of Society	114	❏	❏	❏
10b The Lowdown	119	❏	❏	❏
10b What's Your Function	161	❏	❏	❏
10b White Heat	66	❏	❏	❏
10c Nuts and Bolts	165	❏	❏	❏
10c Mantlepiece	58	❏	❏	❏
10c Shattered Dreams	55	❏	❏	❏
10c Some Assembly Required	165	❏	❏	❏
10d Ass Over Teacups	66	❏	❏	❏
10d Cavorting	147	❏	❏	❏
10d Cling Thing	55	❏	❏	❏
10d Indecision	71	❏	❏	❏
10d Pioneer Route	70	❏	❏	❏
10d Quake and Shake Flakes	171	❏	❏	❏
10d The Fine Line	58	❏	❏	❏
10d The Plague	115	❏	❏	❏
10d Yellow Fever	156	❏	❏	❏
11a Aftershock	112	❏	❏	❏
11a Drama	112	❏	❏	❏
11a Hang Thang	55	❏	❏	❏
11a Hoochie Mama	55	❏	❏	❏
11a Pho King Freeloader	66	❏	❏	❏
11a Ramp Champ 11a/b	171	❏	❏	❏
11a Simple Simon	70	❏	❏	❏
11a Unexpected Difficulties, pitch one	56	❏	❏	❏
11a Walk the Plank	56	❏	❏	❏
11b Rendezvous	71	❏	❏	❏
11c Afterburner	135	❏	❏	❏
11c Angst	92	❏	❏	❏
11c Defamation	111	❏	❏	❏
11c Epiphany	93	❏	❏	❏
11c Handful of Harpies	146	❏	❏	❏
11c Pandora's Box	56	❏	❏	❏
11c Peter Principle	55	❏	❏	❏
11c Valiant Flail to No Avail	171	❏	❏	❏

Routes by Quality

2 Star ★ ★	Page	OS	F	RP
11d Demoralizer	79	❑	❑	❑
11d Force Fed	127	❑	❑	❑
12a Adrenaline	106	❑	❑	❑
12a Bitter Has Been	111	❑	❑	❑
12a Chaste, but Tasty	65	❑	❑	❑
12a Sendsual Feeling	61	❑	❑	❑
12b Diehard	78	❑	❑	❑
12b F.U.B.A.R.	62	❑	❑	❑
12b Funk Flake	122	❑	❑	❑
12b Romper Room	62	❑	❑	❑
12b Scorched Earth	139	❑	❑	❑
12b Tyranny	56	❑	❑	❑
12b Whiplash	55	❑	❑	❑
12c Bottoms Up	63	❑	❑	❑
12c Corruption	169	❑	❑	❑
12c Debut	156	❑	❑	❑
12c Diehard With a Vengeance	79	❑	❑	❑
12c Jeep Jockey	57	❑	❑	❑
12c Master Blaster	79	❑	❑	❑
12c Octo-Mom	66	❑	❑	❑
12c Pimp Chimp	171	❑	❑	❑
12c The Enforcer	57	❑	❑	❑
12c The Forgotten	111	❑	❑	❑
12d All Tapped Out	62	❑	❑	❑
12d Debauchery	169	❑	❑	❑
13a Playing with Fire	114	❑	❑	❑
13a Point Blank	122	❑	❑	❑
13a Seamstress	157	❑	❑	❑
13b Choss Toss	115	❑	❑	❑

3 Star ★ ★ ★	Page	OS	F	RP
5.6 Interplanet Janet	116	❑	❑	❑
10a Made to Order	163	❑	❑	❑
10a Stemsation	169	❑	❑	❑
10b Mass Production	163	❑	❑	❑
10c Gulp Swallow	63	❑	❑	❑

Routes by Quality

3 Star ★ ★ ★

Route	Page	OS	F	RP
10c Manufacturer's Defect	165	❑	❑	❑
10c Quality Control	165	❑	❑	❑
10c Romp	62	❑	❑	❑
10c Utopia	66	❑	❑	❑
10c Wonderstuff	106	❑	❑	❑
10d Assembly Line	165	❑	❑	❑
10d Shockwave	112	❑	❑	❑
11a Chupacabra	169	❑	❑	❑
11a Conundrum	106	❑	❑	❑
11a Delinquency	169	❑	❑	❑
11a Ground Zero	102	❑	❑	❑
11a Peepshow	71	❑	❑	❑
11a Pity Committee	65	❑	❑	❑
11a Short Shot	155	❑	❑	❑
11b American Dream, pitch one	93	❑	❑	❑
11b Atlas	100	❑	❑	❑
11b Double Whammy	105	❑	❑	❑
11b Escape From Agony	171	❑	❑	❑
11b Magic Mushroom	146	❑	❑	❑
11b Maximum Whammy	106	❑	❑	❑
11b Original Sin	140	❑	❑	❑
11b Run Amok	148	❑	❑	❑
11b Salutations	93	❑	❑	❑
11b Swan Song	86	❑	❑	❑
11c American Dream, pitch four	93	❑	❑	❑
11c Fueled by Slander	112	❑	❑	❑
11c Full Conundrum	107	❑	❑	❑
11c Inspiration	79	❑	❑	❑
11c Spunky Monkey	135	❑	❑	❑
11c Synchronicity	65	❑	❑	❑
11d All Washed Up	111	❑	❑	❑
11d Amplified Life	71	❑	❑	❑
11d Déjà vu	93	❑	❑	❑
11d Flying Vee	61	❑	❑	❑
11d Grooverider 2010	101	❑	❑	❑
11d Rocky	148	❑	❑	❑

Routes by Quality

3 Star ★ ★ ★	Page	OS	F	RP
11d Tagger	69	❏	❏	❏
11d Vascular Funk	135	❏	❏	❏
11d Vertical Vee	61	❏	❏	❏
11d Voyeurism	71	❏	❏	❏
12a Block Party	131	❏	❏	❏
12a Block Suppression	133	❏	❏	❏
12a Catch 22	93	❏	❏	❏
12a Character Assassination	155	❏	❏	❏
12a Double Agent	78	❏	❏	❏
12a Double Shock	78	❏	❏	❏
12a Fractional	156	❏	❏	❏
12a Fully Demoralized	79	❏	❏	❏
12a Hand Me Down	155	❏	❏	❏
12a House of Pain	106	❏	❏	❏
12a New Directions	62	❏	❏	❏
12a Romp Direct	62	❏	❏	❏
12a Runaway	148	❏	❏	❏
12a Silver Streaker	125	❏	❏	❏
12a Slander Up	111	❏	❏	❏
12a Spunk	135	❏	❏	❏
12a The View Line	65	❏	❏	❏
12a Winds of Change	79	❏	❏	❏
12b Apocalypse Man	82	❏	❏	❏
12b Apocalypto	82	❏	❏	❏
12b Balrog	92	❏	❏	❏
12b Divine Intervention	130	❏	❏	❏
12b Gravitational Attraction	125	❏	❏	❏
12b Long Shot	155	❏	❏	❏
12b Love	155	❏	❏	❏
12b No Man's Land	140	❏	❏	❏
12b Pith	155	❏	❏	❏
12b Power Surge	121	❏	❏	❏
12b Pucker Power	58	❏	❏	❏
12b Punk's Not Dead	70	❏	❏	❏
12b Purple Haze	148	❏	❏	❏
12b Quarryman	82	❏	❏	❏

Routes by Quality

3 Star ★ ★ ★

Route	Page	OS	F	RP
12b S.F.R.	56	❑	❑	❑
12b Shiver Giver	135	❑	❑	❑
12b Slander Magnet	111	❑	❑	❑
12b Sweet Surrender	102	❑	❑	❑
12b The Enemy Within	127	❑	❑	❑
12b Torture Machine	106	❑	❑	❑
12b Vendetta	87	❑	❑	❑
12c A Sobriquet for Salubrious Slander	101	❑	❑	❑
12c Aggression Suppression	133	❑	❑	❑
12c Bird of Prey	106	❑	❑	❑
12c Buzzkill	78	❑	❑	❑
12c Flawed Perfection	61	❑	❑	❑
12c Funkadelic	137	❑	❑	❑
12c Gollum	92	❑	❑	❑
12c Microquarry	61	❑	❑	❑
12c Procrastination	154	❑	❑	❑
12c Redrum 2010	102	❑	❑	❑
12c Supercruiser	123	❑	❑	❑
12c Toothless Tweaker	154	❑	❑	❑
12c Triple Trouble	87	❑	❑	❑
12c Wages of Sin	140	❑	❑	❑
12d Big Bang	87	❑	❑	❑
12d Cave Troll	92	❑	❑	❑
12d Fractional Envy	156	❑	❑	❑
12d Hysteria	156	❑	❑	❑
12d Love Nest	62	❑	❑	❑
12d Synergy	61	❑	❑	❑
12d Temptation	146	❑	❑	❑
13a Alpha Dog	122	❑	❑	❑
13a Alpha Male	122	❑	❑	❑
13a Burly Boogie	69	❑	❑	❑
13a Control Freak	131	❑	❑	❑
13a Energy Crisis	115	❑	❑	❑
13a Headstrong	130	❑	❑	❑
13a Pith Monster	155	❑	❑	❑
13a Sins of the Flesh	140	❑	❑	❑
13a The Sinner	141	❑	❑	❑

Routes by Quality

3 Star ★ ★ ★	Page	OS	F	RP
13b Crazy Town	153	❑	❑	❑
13b First Born	147	❑	❑	❑
13b Gumption	71	❑	❑	❑
13b Miscreant	101	❑	❑	❑
13b Mojo	93	❑	❑	❑
13b Sweet Agony	169	❑	❑	❑
13b Tattoo	130	❑	❑	❑
13c Debutaunt	156	❑	❑	❑
13c Infinite	156	❑	❑	❑
14b/c Mud Monster	121	❑	❑	❑
Infinite Jest –project	156	❑	❑	❑

4 Star ★ ★ ★ ★	Page	OS	F	RP
5.7 Fun Factory	163	❑	❑	❑
10a Industrial Bliss	164	❑	❑	❑
10b Worker Bee	165	❑	❑	❑
10c Lovely Lady	65	❑	❑	❑
10B Structural Flaw	163	❑	❑	❑
11a Metro	71	❑	❑	❑
11b American Dream, pitch three	93	❑	❑	❑
11b Automatic Static	103	❑	❑	❑
11b Delirious	92	❑	❑	❑
11b Vascular Massacre	135	❑	❑	❑
11c Culture Shock	78	❑	❑	❑
11c Exfoliator	135	❑	❑	❑
11c Salubrious	100	❑	❑	❑
11c Shwazzle Dazzle	153	❑	❑	❑
11d Maximizer	106	❑	❑	❑
11d Pursuit of Pain	87	❑	❑	❑
12a Inspirational Frontiers	79	❑	❑	❑
12a Inspired Change	79	❑	❑	❑
12a Lucky	125	❑	❑	❑
12a New Frontiers	79	❑	❑	❑
12a Survival of the Fittest	101	❑	❑	❑
12a The World Below	120	❑	❑	❑

Routes by Quality

4 Star ★ ★ ★ ★

	Page	OS	F	RP
12b Anger Management	133	❏	❏	❏
12b Exposure	92	❏	❏	❏
12b Infatuation	135	❏	❏	❏
12b Momentum	148	❏	❏	❏
12b Punish the Puppy	56	❏	❏	❏
12b Redneck Agenda	127	❏	❏	❏
12b Redneck Reality	131	❏	❏	❏
12b Solidarity	148	❏	❏	❏
12b Stranger Than Friction	102	❏	❏	❏
12b Swan Hang	86	❏	❏	❏
12b Sweet Static	102	❏	❏	❏
12c American Idiot	125	❏	❏	❏
12c Burning Desire	82	❏	❏	❏
12c Choss Goggles	73	❏	❏	❏
12c Choss Revolution	78	❏	❏	❏
12c Consuming Selection	101	❏	❏	❏
12c Critical Mass	87	❏	❏	❏
12c Nemesis	106	❏	❏	❏
12c Technicolor Tango	107	❏	❏	❏
12c The Shining	102	❏	❏	❏
12c Trepanation	93	❏	❏	❏
12d All That Remains	122	❏	❏	❏
12d Beautiful Disaster	122	❏	❏	❏
12d False Alarm	86	❏	❏	❏
12d Ghetto Fabulous	154	❏	❏	❏
12d Seduction	146	❏	❏	❏
13a Burly Wisdom	69	❏	❏	❏
13a Hands of Time	155	❏	❏	❏
13a Love and Theft	155	❏	❏	❏
13a Power Junkie	131	❏	❏	❏
13a Vertigo	107	❏	❏	❏
13a Weapons of Mass Destruction (W.M.D.)	71	❏	❏	❏
13b Chris Cross	140	❏	❏	❏
13b Energy King	115	❏	❏	❏
13b Tweaker	154	❏	❏	❏
13b Wicked Violator	141	❏	❏	❏

Routes by Quality

4 Star ★ ★ ★ ★	Page	OS	F	RP
13c Consumption	101	❏	❏	❏
13c Lothario	141	❏	❏	❏
13c Seduction Supreme	146	❏	❏	❏

5 Star ★ ★ ★ ★ ★	Page	OS	F	RP
10b Flexercise	82	❏	❏	❏
10c Trundle Trophy	78	❏	❏	❏
10d Tangerine Dream	107	❏	❏	❏
11b Agony Arch	171	❏	❏	❏
11b Flesh and Blood	73	❏	❏	❏
11c Nostalgia	86	❏	❏	❏
11c Violator	141	❏	❏	❏
11d Leviathan	87	❏	❏	❏
12a Forbidden Fruit	146	❏	❏	❏
12a Megalomania	131	❏	❏	❏
12a Raging Raptor	73	❏	❏	❏
12a Swank Nostalgia	86	❏	❏	❏
12b Hanging by a Thread	88	❏	❏	❏
12b The Zone	87	❏	❏	❏
12c Graffiti Wisdom	69	❏	❏	❏
12c Natural Selection	101	❏	❏	❏
12c Sky Pilot	141	❏	❏	❏
12c Taboo	141	❏	❏	❏
12d La Bella Donna	101	❏	❏	❏
12d The Ultimate	86	❏	❏	❏
13a King Pin	115	❏	❏	❏
13a The Saint	140	❏	❏	❏
13b Enigma	130	❏	❏	❏
13c Gypsy	130	❏	❏	❏
10c Mission Possible	140	❏	❏	❏
13c Weight of the World	100	❏	❏	❏
13d Temptation Supreme	146	❏	❏	❏
14b Fusion	140	❏	❏	❏

Index

About The Author	199
Access And Conduct	21
Acknowledgements	6
Adrenaline 12a	106
Afterburner 11c	135
Aftershock 11a	112
Aggression Suppression 12c	133
Agony Arch 11b	171
Agony Arch Area	168
All Tapped Out 13a	62
All That Remains 12d	122
All Washed Up 11d	111
Alpha Dog 13a	122
Alpha Male 13a	122
Amenities	18
American Dream 11b, 10a, 11b, 11c	93
American Idiot 12c	125
Amplified Life 11d	71
Anger Management 12b	133
Anger Management Area	133
Angst 11c	92
Apocalypse Man 12b	82
Apocalypto 12b	82
Approach Pitch 5.7	61
Area History	37
A Sobriquet for Salubrious Slander 12c	101
Ass Over Teacups 10d	66
Assembly Line 10d	165
Atlas 11b H	100
Automatic Static 11b	103
Baby Brigade 12b	66
Baby Face 10b	111
Balrog 12b	92
Beautiful Disaster 12d	122
Big Bang 12d	87
Bird of Prey 12c	106
Bitter Has Been 12a	111
Block Party 12a	131
Block Suppression 12a	133
Bottom Feeder 11b	58
Bottoms Up 12c	63
Burly Boogie 13a	69
Burly Wisdom 13a	69
Burning Desire 12c	82
Burnout 11c	114
Buzzkill 12c	78
Catch 22 12a	93
Cave Troll 12d (r)	92
Cavorting 10d	147
Character Assassination 12a	155
Chas' Route 11c	58
Chaste, but Tasty 12a	65
Choss Goggles 12c	73
Choss Revolution 12c	78
Choss Toss 13b	115
Chris Cross 13b	140
Chupacabra 11a	169
Cling Thing 10d	55
Conjunction Junction 5.9	159
Consuming Selection 12c	101
Consumption 13c	101
Control Freak 13a	131
Conundrum 11a	106
Cornered 11d	157
Corruption 12c	169
Crazy Town 13b	153
Critical Mass 12c	87
Cruiser 10d	122
Culture Shock 11c	78
Debauchery 12d	169
Debut 12c	156
Debutaunt 13c	156
Defamation 11c	111
Déjà vu 11d	93
Delinquency 11a	169
Delirious 11b	92
Demoralizer 11d	79
Developer Profiles	47
Diagonal Direct 11a	55
Diehard 12b	78
Diehard with a Vengeance 12c	79
Disco Inferno 10c	114
Divine Intervention 12b	130
Doctor Greenthumb 10b	157
Dollars and Sense 5.7	159
Double Agent 12a	78
Double Shock 12a	78
Double Whammy 11b	105
Drama 11a	112
Energy Crisis 13a	115
Energy King 13b	115
Enigma 13b	130
Epiphany 11c	93
Escape from Agony 11b	171

Index

Escape from Agony 11b	168
Every Dog Has His Day	169
Excuse Abuse 10a	70
Exfoliator 11c	135
Exposure 12b (r)	92
F.U.B.A.R. 12b	62
False Alarm 12d	86
Fear the Smear 5.8	171
Feetal Rearrangement 5.8, 10c, A2	58
Fiasco 11c	115
First Born 13b	147
Flake and Bake 5.8	114
Flawed Perfection 12c	61
Flesh and Blood 11b	73
Flexercise 10b	82
Flying Vee 11d	61
Forbidden Fruit 12a	146
Force Fed 11d	127
Fractional 12a	156
Fractional Envy 12d	156
Fueled by Slander 11c	112
Full Conundrum 11c	107
Fully Demoralized 12a	79
Fun Factory 5.7	163
Function Junction 5.9	161
Funk Flake 12b	122
Funkadelic 12c	137
Fusion 14b	140
Ghetto Fabulous 12d	154
Gollum 12c	92
Goody Two Shoes 10b	58
Graffiti Wisdom 12c	69
Grandma Seizure 11b	61
Gravitational Attraction 12b	125
Groove Factor 5.9	66
Grooverider 2010 11d	101
Ground Zero 11a	102
Gulp Swallow 10c	63
Gumption 13b	71
Gypsy 13c	130
Hand Me Down 12a	155
Handful of Harpies 11c	146
Hands of Time 13a	155
Hang Thang 11a	55
Hanging by a Thread 12b	88
Headstrong 13a	130
Hercules Hand Crack 5.8	78
Hoochie Mama 11a	55
House of Cards 10b	161
House of Pain 12a	106
Hump or Dump 10a	171
Hysteria 12d	156
I'm Just a Bill 5.6	159
Indecision 10d	71
Industrial Bliss 10a	164
Infatuation 12b	135
Infinite 13c	156
Infinite Jest – project	156
Inspiration 11c	79
Inspirational Frontiers 12a	79
Inspired Change 12a	79
Interplanet Janet 5.6	161
Jaunt 10b	115
Jeep Jockey 12c	57
Juggernaut 12b	66
King Pin 13a	115
La Bella Donna 12d	101
Leapfrog 5.9	119
Left of the Roof	72
Leviathan 11d	87
Location And Driving Times	12
Long Shot 12b	155
Lothario 13c	141
Love 12b	155
Love and Theft 13a	155
Love Nest 12d	62
Lovely Lady 10c	65
Lowrider 10b	119
Lowrider Direct 10b	121
Lucky 12a	125
Made to Order 10a	163
Magic Mushroom 11b	146
Mantle Marathon 10a	57
Mantlepiece 10c	58
Manufacturer's Defect 10c	165
Marathon Man 11b	57
Mass Production 10b	163
Master Blaster 12c	79
Maximizer 11d	106
Maximum Whammy 11b	100
Megalomania 12a	101
Metro 11a	71
Metro Sector	69
Microquarry 12c	01

Climber's Guide: Riverside Quarry • 185

Index

Minimizer 10a	105
Miscreant 13b	101
Mission Possible 13c	140
Mojo 13b	93
Momentum 12b	148
Mud Monster 14b/c	121
Mud Ramp 10a	122
Mudslinger 11d	112
My Hero Zero 5.0	159
Natural Selection 12c	101
Nemesis 12c	106
New Directions 12a	62
New Frontiers 12a	79
No Man's Land 12b	140
Nostalgia 11c	86
Nuts and Bolts 10c	165
Octo-Mom 12c	66
One for the Road 5.8 (r)	66
Open Project 5.15 ? q	141
Original Sin 11b	140
Pandora's Box 11c	56
Peepshow 11a	71
Peter Principle 11c	55
Pho King Freeloader 11a	66
Pigeon, the Other White Meat 10c	55
Pimp Chimp 12c	171
Pioneer Route 10d	70
Pith 12b	155
Pith Monster 13a	155
Pity Committee 11a	65
Planned Obsolescence 5.9	163
Playing with Fire 13a	114
Pleasure Dome 10b	67
Point Blank 13a	122
Power Junkie 13a	131
Power Play 10b	105
Power Surge 12b	121
Prisoner of Society 10b	114
Procrastination 12c	154
Pucker Power 12b (r)	58
Punish the Puppy 12b	56
Punk's Not Dead 12b	70
Purple Haze 12b	148
Pursuit of Pain 11d	87
Quake and Shake Flakes 10d	171
Quality Control 10c	165
Quarry Grade Dozens	172
Quarry Routes By Quality	174
Quarryman 12b	82
Raging Raptor 12a	73
Ramp Champ 11a	171
Redneck Agenda 12b	127
Redneck Reality 12b	131
Redrum 2010 12c	102
Rendezvous 11b	71
Right of the Roof	98
Rocky 11d	148
Romp 10c	62
Romp Direct 12a	62
Romper Room 12b	62
Roof Area	83
Rubble Row	113
Run Amok 11b	148
Runaway 12a	148
S.F.R. 12b H	56
Salubrious 11c	100
Salutations 11b	93
Schoolhouse Rock	158
Schoolhouse Rock 5.8	159
Scorched Earth 12b	139
Scrawny, not Brawny 10a	65
Seamstress 13a	157
Seduction 12d	146
Seduction Supreme 13c	146
Sendsual Feeling 12a	61
Shattered Dreams 10c	55
Shiver Giver 12b	135
Shockwave 10d	112
Short Shot 11a	155
Shwazzle Dazzle 11c	153
Sika Soldier 12c	115
Silver Streaker 12a	125
Simple Simon 11a	70
Sins of the Flesh 13a	140
Six Sigma Certified 10b	165
Sky Pilot 12c	141
Slab City	52
Slab City Center	60
Slab City Left	54
Slab City Right	64
Slander Magnet 12b	111
Slander Sector	110
Slander Up 12a	111
Slide Zone	121

Index

Solidarity 12b	148	The World Below 12a	125
Some Assembly Required 10c	165	The Zone 12b	87
Spitfire 12b	139	Tiptoe 5.7	122
Spunk 12a	135	Toothless Tweaker 12c	154
Spunky Monkey 11c	135	Torture Machine 12b	106
Stem Job 11a	169	Torture Machine Area	105
Stemsation 10a	169	Trepanation 12c	93
Stranger than Friction 12b	102	Triple Trouble 12c	87
Structural Flaw 10b	163	Trundle Trophy 10c	78
Supercruiser 12c	123	Tweaker 13b	154
Survival of the Fittest 12a	101	Tyrannosaurus Debt 5.9	159
Swan Hang 12b	86	Tyranny 12b	56
Swan Song 11b	86	Unexpected Difficulties 11a, 11b	56
Swank Nostalgia 12a	86	Union Man 11a	165
Sweet Agony 13b	169	Utopia 10c	66
Sweet Static 12b	102	Valiant Flail to No Avail 11c	171
Sweet Surrender 12b	102	Vascular Funk 11d	135
Synchronicity 11c	65	Vascular Massacre 11b	135
Synergy 12d H	61	Vendetta 12b	87
Taboo Area	139	Vertical Vee 11d, 5.8 q	61
Taboo 12c	141	Vertigo 13a	107
Tagger 11d	69	Victim of Gravity 10a	161
Tailspin 10a	119	Victim of Reality 10a	114
Tangerine Dream 10d	107	Violator 11c	141
Tattoo 13b	130	Voyeurism 11d	71
Taxman Max 5.5	159	Wages of Sin 12c	140
Technicolor Tango 12c	107	Walk the Plank 11a	56
Temptation 12d	146	Weapons of Mass Destruction	
Temptation Supreme 13d	146	(W.M.D.) 13a	71
The Alcove	153	Weather And Season	17
The Check's in the Mail 5.7	159	Weight of the World 13c	100
The Degenerate 12b	169	Whammy 10a	105
The Enemy Within 12b	127	What's Your Function? 10b	161
The Energy Blues 5.6	159	Whiplash 12b	55
The Enforcer 12c	57	White Heat 10b	66
The Fine Line 10d	58	White Light 5.7	67
The Forgotten 12c	111	Wicked Violator 5.13b	141
The Fun Factory	162	Wildlife	16
The Lowdown 10b	119	Winds of Change 12a	79
The Plague 10d	115	Wonderstuff 10c	106
The Saint 13a	140	Worker Bee 10b	165
The Shield	127	Yellow Fever 10d	156
The Shining 12c	102		
The Sinner 13a	141		
The Tall Wall	124		
The Ultimate 12d	86		
The View Line 12a	65		

Climber's Guide: Riverside Quarry • 187

The Factory
Bouldering

Building Better Climbers

**Southern California's
Premiere Bouldering Facility**

THEFACTORYBOULDERING.COM

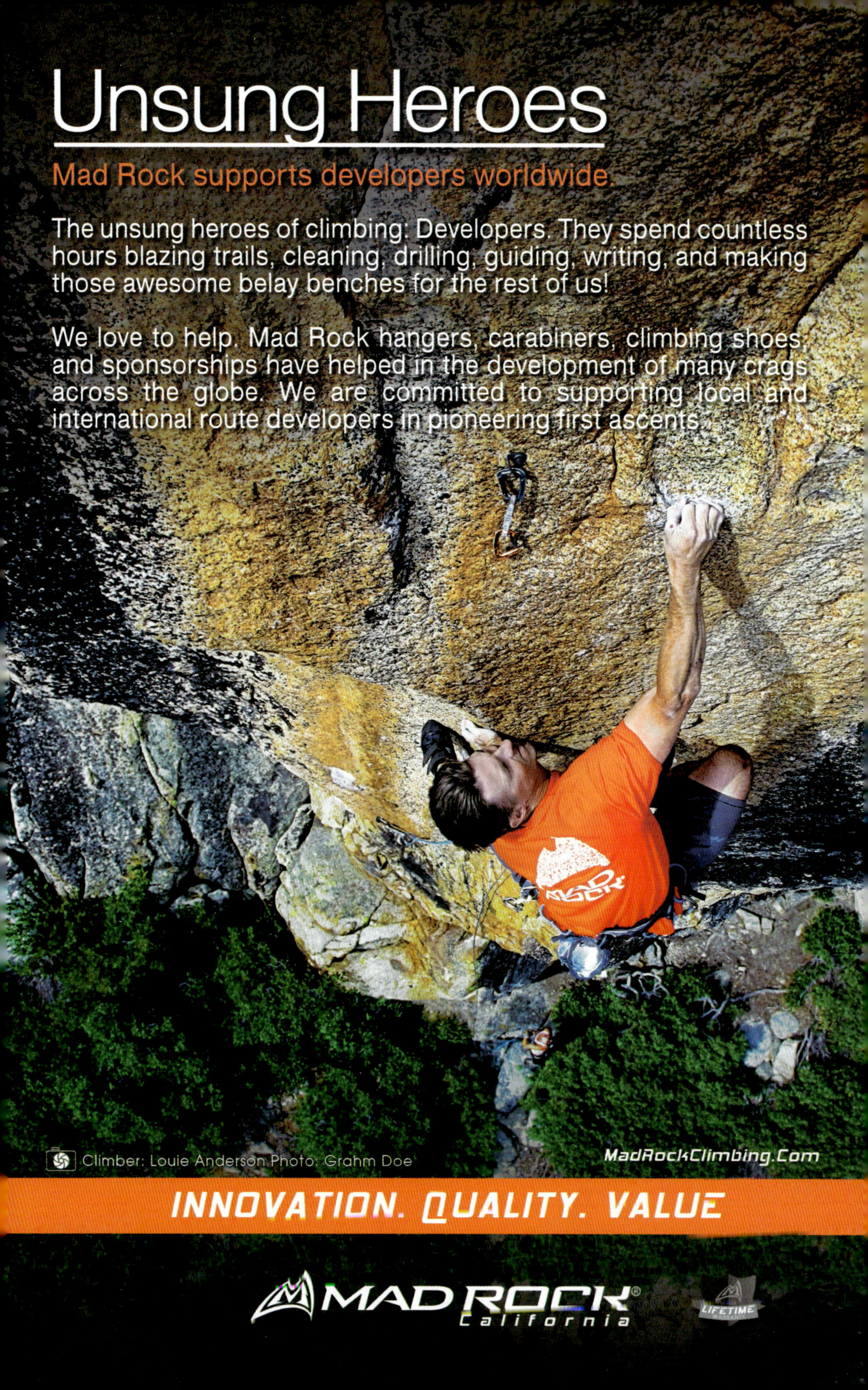

Unsung Heroes

Mad Rock supports developers worldwide.

The unsung heroes of climbing: Developers. They spend countless hours blazing trails, cleaning, drilling, guiding, writing, and making those awesome belay benches for the rest of us!

We love to help. Mad Rock hangers, carabiners, climbing shoes, and sponsorships have helped in the development of many crags across the globe. We are committed to supporting local and international route developers in pioneering first ascents.

Climber: Louie Anderson Photo: Grahm Doe

MadRockClimbing.Com

INNOVATION. QUALITY. VALUE

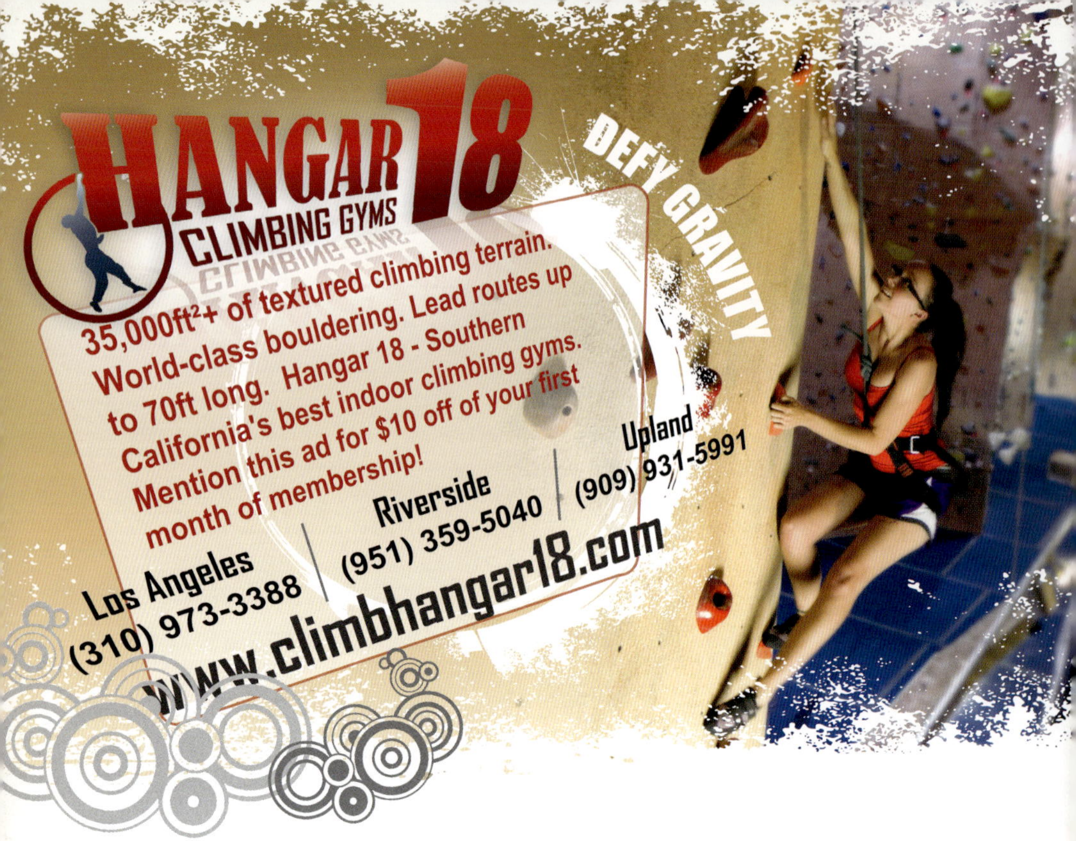
HANGAR 18
CLIMBING GYMS
DEFY GRAVITY
35,000ft²+ of textured climbing terrain. World-class bouldering. Lead routes up to 70ft long. Hangar 18 - Southern California's best indoor climbing gyms. Mention this ad for $10 off of your first month of membership!
Los Angeles
(310) 973-3388
Riverside
(951) 359-5040
Upland
(909) 931-5991
www.climbhangar18.com

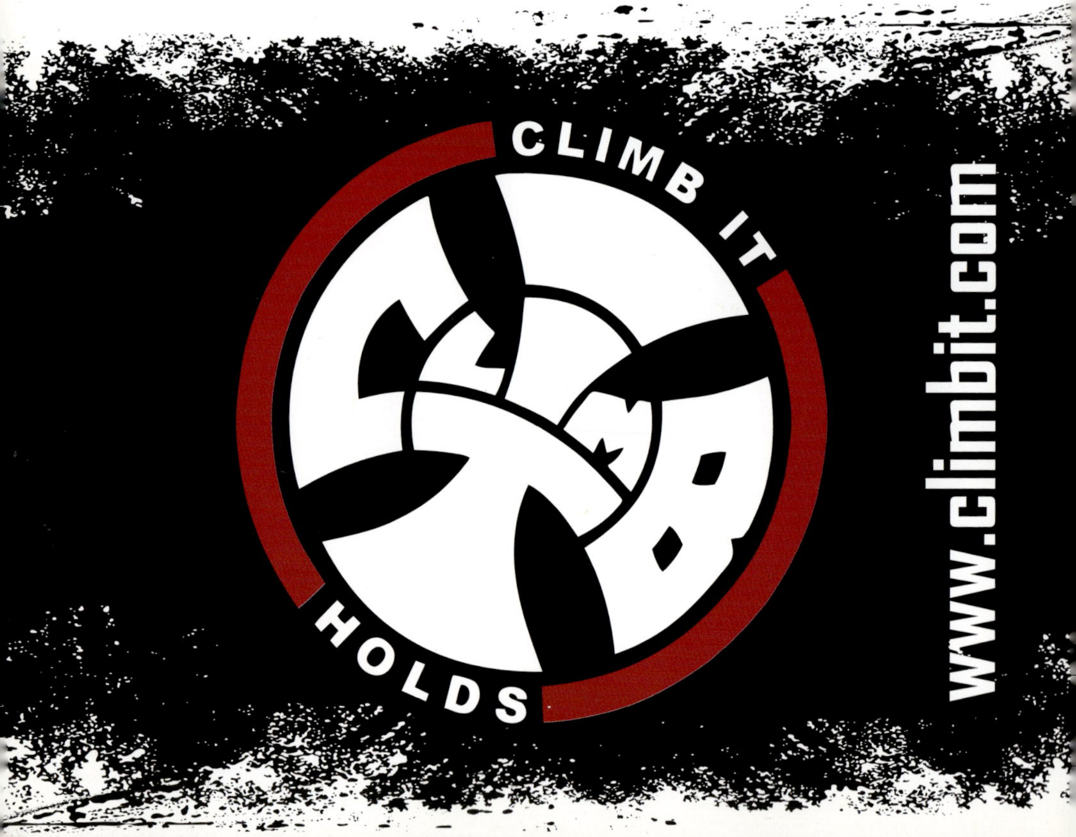
CLIMB IT
HOLDS
www.climbit.com

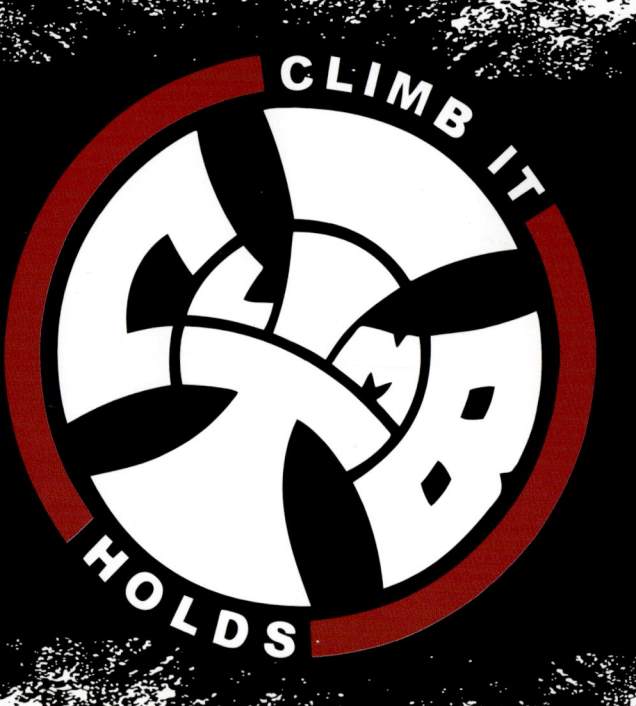

WHAT IF
FEAR OF LIABILITY RUNS AMOK?

Protect America's Climbing

CLIMB IN SAN DIEGO COUNTY

CORTE MADERA · EL CAJON MOUNTAIN · EAGLE PEAK

THE SAN DIEGO CLIMBER'S **POCKET GUIDE**

WWW.ALLIEDCLIMBERS.ORG

Multi-pitch climbing is right down the road
ACSD Pocket Guide available online

Keli Balo on pitch 5 of *Smooth Sailing* (.11c), Corte Madera

ALLIED CLIMBERS OF SAN DIEGO

FUSION

MADE HERE

USED HERE

www.fusionclimb.com

EMPOWER
Community

- Local Events and Community Outreach
- Youth and Adult Programs
- 10 Minutes from the Quarry

THRESHOLD
CLIMBING + FITNESS GYM

www.climbth.com   2111 Iowa Ave Unit A Riverside, CA

The perfect meal for after your climbing adventures.

Visit us at 3612 Valley Way

Lead Cave

Boulder Cave

VERTICAL HOLD
Sport Climbing Inc.

San Diego's Finest Indoor Climbing Gym

24,000 sq ft. textured walls
150+ toprope routes on 40 ropes
100+ lead routes
250+ boulder problems
Professional setting staff
New routes set every week
Campus and hang boards
12ft tall system board

Full amenities and locker rooms
Free yoga Tuesday & Thursday
Free monthly clinics
Observation deck for events
Live DJ every Monday
Free wireless internet
Birthday parties & overnight events

9580 Distribution Ave, San Diego, CA 92121 - (858) 586-7572

Topout Boulder

WORKOUT. HANGOUT. CLIMB ON.

Come challenge your body and mind at **Orange County's first indoor bouldering gym.** Suitable for all experience levels, our gym features a 15-foot top out, 16-foot cave, and an assortment of frequently changing climbing routes. At TruHold, we strive to not only provide climbers with a top-quality bouldering workout, but also take pride in our modern facilities and inviting atmosphere.

For more information, visit:
TruHoldClimbing.com
or email us at: info@truholdclimbing.com

23812 Via Fabricante • Mission Viejo, CA 92691

EXERCISE YOUR MIND AND BODY!
WWW.ROCKCITYCLIMBING.COM
714-777-4884

Rock City

HIGH ROPES COURSE

- TEAM BUILDING
- INSTRUCTION
- ADVENTURE RACING
- TRAINING
- SCOUTS
- PARTIES
- CAMPS

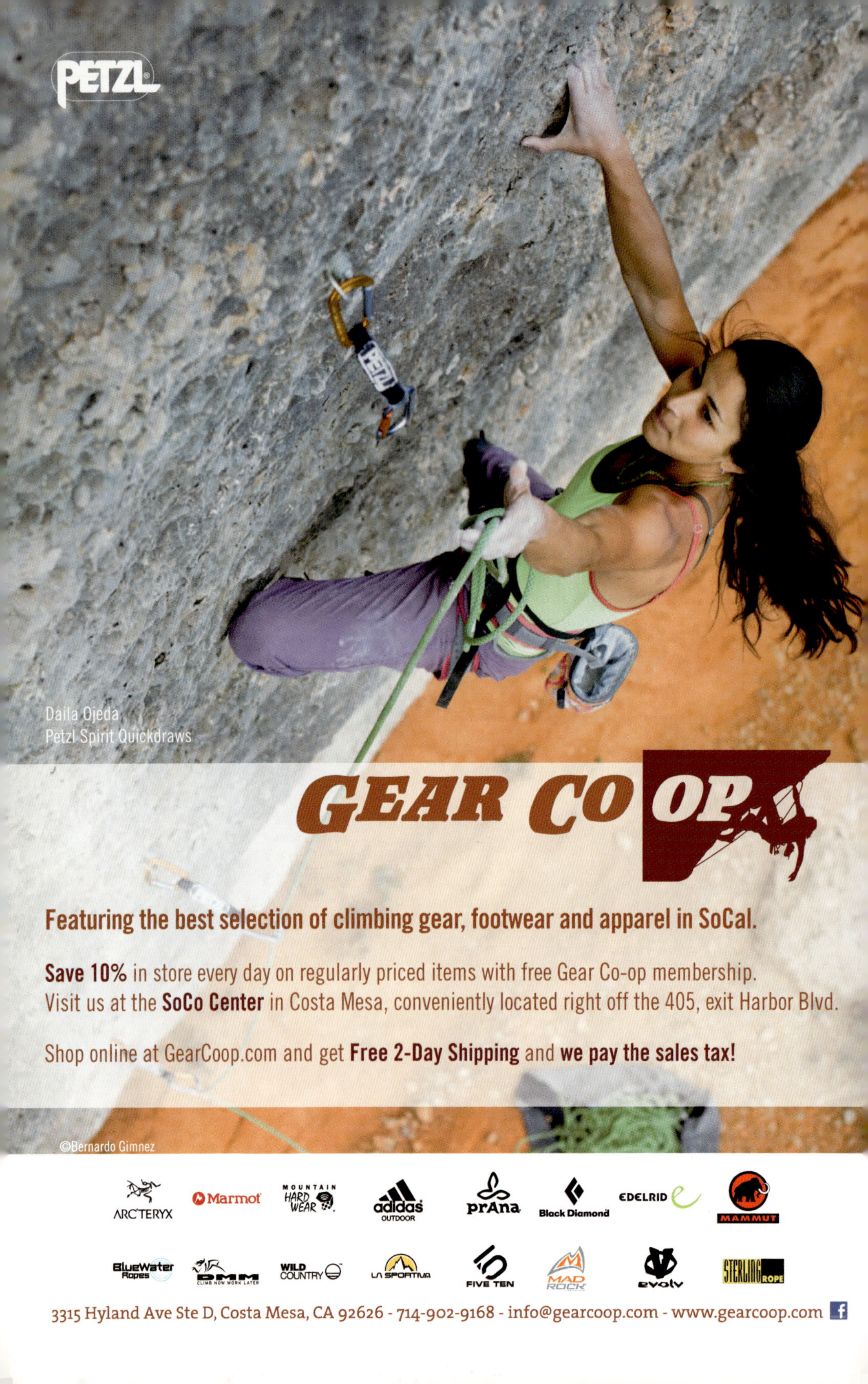
PETZL
Daila Ojeda
Petzl Spirit Quickdraws
GEAR CO OP
Featuring the best selection of climbing gear, footwear and apparel in SoCal.
Save 10% in store every day on regularly priced items with free Gear Co-op membership.
Visit us at the SoCo Center in Costa Mesa, conveniently located right off the 405, exit Harbor Blvd.
Shop online at GearCoop.com and get Free 2-Day Shipping and we pay the sales tax!
©Bernardo Gimnez
ARC'TERYX
Marmot
MOUNTAIN HARD WEAR
adidas OUTDOOR
prAna
Black Diamond
EDELRID
MAMMUT
BlueWater Ropes
DMM CLIMB NOW WORK LATER
WILD COUNTRY
LA SPORTIVA
FIVE TEN
MAD ROCK
evolv
STERLING ROPE
3315 Hyland Ave Ste D, Costa Mesa, CA 92626 - 714-902-9168 - info@gearcoop.com - www.gearcoop.com

About The Author

Louie Anderson has been climbing since the age of eight, having been introduced to the sport through a friend of his father. In the years since, he has enjoyed many different aspects of the sport; from bouldering to big walls to overseas sport climbing. However, Louie's main interest lies in new routes. Whether it be hunting for new areas or establishing new routes at existing areas, this aspect of our sport is what fuels his motivation. He established many of the routes in this guide and was also a prime developer at Santa Monica Mountain areas such as Echo Cliffs and Boney Bluff, as well as the San Bernardino Mountain areas of Frustration Creek, Rocky Hollow and the Mill Creek Wash. Other So Cal areas have samplings of his routes, as do regional areas in California, Nevada, Arizona, Utah, and Baja California.

Aside from his new route related labors, Louie works as a Project Manager for the construction industry, and has his own climbing wall construction company. He also designs artificial climbing holds for several companies. Louie has two daughters: Kayla and Madison, ages 18 and 15, and lives in a rural area of Orange County, California, in a house that he built himself.

The author welcomes all input on difficulty or quality ratings, new routes, or any other comments pertinent to the information provided in this book. He can be reached via email at louieanderson@live.com. Feel free to contact him as often as you like (even after every visit if you desire) with comments. The information provided in this book is only as accurate as the information and opinions offered by area users.

Make a Difference

You Can Make a Difference

More so than other climbing areas, the routes at The Quarry demand maintenance. Due to the blasting history of the cliff, it transfers the ground's constant movement in a variety of unpredictable ways. Originally solid holds become loose (or looser) and reinforced holds have their epoxy crack and fail. Keeping the crag's routes safe and secure can sometimes require a lot of effort and associated cost.

Further, the fact that people continue to dump trash on the property demands regular clean-up efforts by the climbing community to keep the area looking as good as it can.

If you would like to help out with ongoing efforts to address these and other area concerns, please contact the author at either louieanderson@live.com or PO Box 411, Silverado, California 92676-0411. He will keep you informed on planned clean up and trail maintenance events.

Willard Gove on Technicolor Tango (12c)
Photo: Richard Heinrich

If you would rather contribute financially to these efforts, your donation can be made to either the email or mailing address shown above.

Either way, your assistance is greatly appreciated. Together we can all keep the area safer, cleaner and more enjoyable for all who visit.